Called Out but Safe

al CLARK

SAFE!

I ALWAYS SAID YOU WUZ FAIR, AL!

CONSIDERED TO BE ONE OF THE FAIREST AND MOST IMPARTIAL UMPIRES OF HIS GENERATION, LARGER-THAN-LIFE AL CLARK LOGGED AN AMAZING 26-YEAR MAJOR LEAGUE CAREER THAT SPANNED 1976-2001. THE SON OF TRENTON SPORTSWRITER HERB CLARK, AL ONCE THREW HIS DAD OUT OF THE YANKEE STADIUM CLUBHOUSE WHILE STILL NEEDING TO RIDE HOME WITH HIM!

YOU'RE OUTTA HERE, DAD... BUT WAIT FOR ME IN THE CAR!

AL IS THE ONLY JEWISH UMPIRE IN AMERICAN LEAGUE HISTORY.

AL WAS ON THE FIELD FOR MANY HISTORIC GAMES, INCLUDING CAL RIPKEN'S RECORD-SETTING STREAK GAME, NOLAN RYAN'S 300TH WIN, AND THE BUCKY DENT GAME, TO NAME A FEW. AL RAN AFOUL WITH THE LAW IN A MEMORABILIA SCANDAL THAT LANDED HIM IN PRISON FOR A BRIEF TIME, BUT HE ADMITTED HIS MISTAKE, ACCEPTED FULL RESPONSIBILITY, AND MOVED ON. "I WAS ALWAYS DEEMED TO BE VERY FAIR," AL SAYS OF HIS YEARS UMPING, "BUT DON'T SCREW WITH ME, BECAUSE BY VIRTUE OF THE UNIFORM I WEAR, I WILL WIN!"

Called Out but Safe

A Baseball Umpire's Journey

AL CLARK *with* DAN SCHLOSSBERG

Foreword by Marty Appel

University of Nebraska Press | *Lincoln and London*

Library of Congress Cataloging-in-Publication Data
Clark, Al, 1948–
Called out but safe: a baseball umpire's journey / Al
Clark with Dan Schlossberg; foreword by Marty Appel.
pages   cm
ISBN 978-0-8032-4688-1 (cloth: alk. paper)—ISBN
978-0-8032-5496-1 (pdf)—ISBN 978-0-8032-5497-8
(epub)—ISBN 978-0-8032-5498-5 (mobi) 1. Clark, Al,
1948– 2. Baseball umpires—United States—
Biography. I. Schlossberg, Dan, 1948– II. Title.
GV865.C4365A3 2014
796.357092—dc23
[B]
2013046023

Set in Minion Pro by Renni Johnson.
Designed by A. Shahan.

In April of 1999 my mom, Shirley, passed away. With my dad, Herb, still very much alive then, that was my first experience at losing a parent. Usually at a parent's funeral, the regrets heard in a eulogy from a son or daughter are, "I wish I would have told them how much I loved them," or, "I wish I could have made them proud." The truth is both of them knew how much I loved them, and I know how proud they were of me.

During my mom's eulogy, my brother Jeff mentioned one regret that rang true for all three of her sons: "Mom taught us how to hit a baseball and Dad taught us how to drive." We really wish it had been the other way around. For sure, that is our *only* regret. My parents were not only wonderful and loving but true lifelong friends.

Mom and Dad, thank you for mapping the road to an amazing and blessed life. This book is dedicated to your loving memory.

AL CLARK

My parents were my inspiration too. As an only child, I could have inherited my dad's radiology practice in the skyscraper (and the only remaining Art Deco building) in downtown Passaic, New Jersey. But that was not to be—not for a boy who found writing a breeze but struggled with math and science courses. Against their advice to pursue law (because I was so argumentative) or some other lucrative occupation, I chose journalism, the only career that could bring me into a baseball world I could not attain as an athlete.

I still remember my dad talking about watching Carl Hubbell and the New York Giants in the Polo Grounds. And I remember watching the 1957 World Series with him on a black-and-white Zenith with the sound turned off. His quiet but detailed explanations turned me into a fan.

Had that not happened, I never would have met Al Clark, who will be a cherished friend for life.

So thanks again, Miriam and Ezra, for putting up with a boy's dreams and helping him realize them. My work on this book is dedicated to you. I only wish you were here to read it.

DAN SCHLOSSBERG

Contents

Foreword

When people talk about "inside baseball" or "the inner game," they're referring to what's really happening on the field while the fans in the stands and even the media members sit clueless as to the hidden intrigue.

Most players have histories with opponents. Perhaps an altercation might have taken place while they were in the Minors or in high school or college. Maybe some score was left unsettled. Or some wild night on the town forever bonded the two souls suddenly facing each other.

Player-umpire relationships are like that, too. They've always intrigued me.

For one thing, how do players, coaches, and managers learn the names of the umpires? Umps are seldom announced, even though their names usually appear on the scoreboard before a game. Rookies are rarely introduced to umpires, as in "Choo Choo, meet Augie Donatelli!" But players do learn umpire names, grunt out greetings, and on occasion even hear, "He's a straight shooter. He gives you a lot of space to make your point, he's not trigger-happy, and he calls a good game." Occasionally.

More often, players and umpires have a *Minor* League history that isn't fully forgotten.

Players hear that so-and-so is a "terrible umpire" and the reason they're hitting .211 is the fault of an umpire with a ridiculous excuse for a strike zone. Sort of like the reason you've had your license suspended three times is that the cops are picking on you when you're *only* driving ninety-one miles per hour.

Smart players learn umpires' names.

Al Clark was easy because his first name was on his cap. When the leagues had distinct umpiring crews, Al worked for the American League and his hat read AL.

He also wore glasses. Good grief. The single biggest point of ridicule for old-time umps was the suggestion by managers or players that the culprit couldn't see straight—it was unheard of for any ump to be caught dead in glasses.

Unlike players, whose reflexes start to fade around the age of forty, umpires often last decades longer. I can only imagine how those old-time umpires must have dreaded the aging process, when a little lens assistance would surely have been welcome. Al Clark not only wore glasses and had his name on his head, but was the son of the only form of human life players consider lower than an umpire: a sportswriter. And did I mention he was Jewish?

Herb Clark, a gifted journalist with the Trenton (New Jersey) newspapers, covered the Yankees from a perch in the Yankee Stadium press box. As the team's public relations director, I sat next to him on many occasions and heard of his love of the game in general and the Yankees in particular. Herb knew his stuff, knew the history, and was an engaging fellow with whom to watch a game.

When Al Clark made his umpiring debut at Yankee Stadium, I poked Herb in the ribs and joked, "Any relation?"

"Yeah," he said. "He's my son."

You could have knocked me over with a ball-and-strike indicator.

"You have a son who's an umpire?" I asked. "A *Major League* umpire?"

All of us in the press box started paying special attention to Herb's son, who went on to work in the Majors. A solid professional, he led the tough life of a sports official, both enamored of the glamor of the big leagues and cautiously distancing himself from it.

I learned from Eric Gregg, the gregarious National League umpire with whom I wrote a book, what a lonely life an ump could lead. He traveled in groups of four, never mixed with players, and had few friends in each city—if he had any at all. He hoped to do his job in relative obscurity because that was a sign of nothing having gone wrong.

At the ends of their careers, umpires tend to be measured by the big games in which they appeared, even if they had little to do with those history-making events. They are also measured by the postseason and All-Star games for which they are selected—often by seniority or rotation.

They are treated well in the box scores, where their first and last names are listed. Players see only their last names.

Players also see how to behave—or risk ejection by the umpires. Our man Al was rather conservative, tossing only sixty-five offenders in the course of twenty-six years, but one of those offenders was the mild-mannered Cal Ripken Jr. He'll tell you what happened later in this book.

The ultimate measure of an umpire is the character of the man and the day-to-day respect he earned within his profession. Al honed his craft well and served baseball nobly for a long time. He was well regarded by his peers—even though he was among those whose strike calls never sounded like the word "strike."

Shortly after he retired his whiskbroom, Al endured a character bump, a surprising anticlimax that he covers here with admirable honesty. His is a story of triumph, error, and rebirth. He gives us a revealing glimpse into those who get us through those 54 outs each day so that the game can be inscribed into the pages of baseball history.

Finally let me say a word about my friend Dan Schlossberg, Al's coauthor on this work. The pairing of Schlossberg and Clark is the best match I've seen since a guy named Lewis took another Clark to explore America together.

Dan has always been an astute observer of the game, whether writing books with players, broadcasters, or umpires or just chronicling the game's charm through assorted compendia of literature. His *Baseball Catalog* and *Baseball Book of Why* will always stand as important reference books for things not found elsewhere. Dan had just the right curiosity to draw out Al's fascinating story.

Together they've given us an intriguing look at a side of the game we seldom see.

MARTY APPEL

Preface

Al Clark and I are so much alike that it's frightening.

Two Jewish kids from New Jersey, we weren't good enough to play baseball. But we loved the game so much that we found other means of reaching the Major Leagues and rubbing elbows with the stars we idolized. In fact, sometimes we rubbed them the wrong way.

Al and I are affable but outspoken individuals who march to the beat of a different drummer. We love to laugh and shared many comical moments as we collaborated on this book. That's especially true because Al is an umpire who fancies himself a writer, whereas I am a writer who loves to make the snap decisions required of an umpire—and to defend them when an argument ensues.

The project took well over a year, from the time fellow author Marty Appel and literary agent Rob Wilson introduced us at Foley's New York to the excruciating (for me) word-by-word revision of the chapters I sent to Al for review. Suffice to say that we did not always concur, just as we had friendly but heated disagreements during the 2012 political campaign. All I can say is it's a good thing Al has a loud voice—honed by years of bellowing at such notorious umpire baiters as Billy Martin, Earl Weaver, and Dick Williams.

I must confess that Al Clark taught me more about the game in a year than I had learned in forty-four years as a denizen of the baseball press box.

I had no idea, for example, that every game I watch involves *three* teams: the visitor, the home team, and the umpiring crew.

Nor did I know umpires, like pitchers and catchers, used signals to communicate during games.

Al Clark was no ordinary umpire. In fact, he was one of a kind.

He lasted twenty-six years in the Majors, long enough to rank ninth in career games umpired, and officiated in Nolan Ryan's three-hundredth win, Randy Johnson's first no-hitter, Cal Ripken's record-breaker, and the sudden-death playoff game punctuated by Bucky Dent's home run.

He worked the World Series that was stopped by an earthquake, survived an Oklahoma tornado, watched Mount St. Helens erupt, and took a fan to court for dousing him with beer after a game.

He also wondered whether Venezuelan Winter League fans were serious when they yelled, "Kill the umpire!"

A genuinely nice guy with a heart of gold, Al loves kids, animals, and golf even more than he once loved wine, women, and song. He even offered to chisel a fake golf club while he was incarcerated for four months following a post-career snafu but was turned down because the warden thought a fellow inmate might reshape it into a spear.

His life has been a true roller-coaster ride. The son of a sportswriter I knew during my days at the Associated Press (AP), Al tried his hand at teaching and writing before realizing he would rather eat steak than hamburger. Umpiring, which he tried and enjoyed as a second summer job while in high school, seemed like a viable alternative with a better ceiling—if he succeeded against enormous odds.

He had already mastered the difficult art of blowing the shofar on the High Holy Days, so what could be so difficult about learning the baseball rule book and executing the art of umpiring? After finishing umpire school and a four-year tenure in the Minors, he proved he was ready.

In the pages that follow, Al reveals how he intimidated Andruw Jones into signing autographs, why he ejected Frank Robinson during the National Anthem, and what his dad, Herb, said that got him thrown out of the umpires' room at Yankee Stadium.

I hope you'll enjoy reading this book as much as I enjoyed putting it together.

DAN SCHLOSSBERG

Acknowledgments

To acknowledge so many individuals in so little space is an impossible task for someone fortunate enough to live the life I've enjoyed.

My brothers Jeffrey and Marty, the late Al Rossi, and my lifelong friend Phil Moran never withheld their friendship or loyalty, even during the darkest of times.

Friends in the travel industry and professionals in the air, car, hotel, and restaurant business are invaluable to a road warrior. They include Mark Stephen (USAir), Tim Wilson (United), Bobby Troitino (Advantage Car Rental), Paul Kennedy (The Olympic Club), Mike Jorgensen (Westin), Randy Wilcott (Mandarin International), Paul Scott, Corky Campisi (Campisi's Egyptian of Dallas), and former hospitality executives Bob White and Sheryl DeWalt, whose friendship I've enjoyed for decades.

George Molinari from Chicago made sure umpires had transportation to and from airports and around town.

My Williamsburg family of Al Klapperich, Woody Woolwine, Mike Mitchell, Buddy Dacus, Lou Carducci, Jerry Prosek, and Diane Knights made the off-season as worthwhile and fun as the regular baseball season. The same goes for my business partner E. J. (Red) McGarry, who made it possible to launch Ump's Eye View, a public-relations company whose name I conceived.

Although some people consider attorneys necessary evils, my brothers and I are honored to retain a family lawyer who is also a friend. I don't know what I would have done without Richard D. Meadow of the Lanier Law Firm. He's honest, fair, and trustworthy. It doesn't get any better than that.

Kudos also to foreword writer and publicist Marty Appel, a friend throughout my professional career, who had the foresight to pair me with coauthor Dan Schlossberg. What a stroke of genius! Our project has taken more than a year to complete, but not a day passed when Dan did *not* work with passion, patience, and diligence while adding his unbelievable expertise and knowledge.

Finally, thanks to my professional brothers—the umpires—who added to what was a tremendous career for thirty years. I can only hope and pray that some of my wit, wisdom, and guidance have been helpful to them on and off the field. Just as established umpires helped me from my early years forward, I have always tried to help my younger brethren in blue (even though they aren't always "the men in blue" anymore).

To my closest umpire brother, Rick Reed, I can say only, "I love ya, man."

To each and every person previously named, I sincerely say, "Thank you." I wouldn't be half the person I am today had it not been for your friendship, loyalty, and guidance.

AL CLARK

This book would not have been possible without longtime friend and fellow baseball author Marty Appel, who previously matched me with a celebrity partner in Ron Blomberg. Marty is not only quite skilled at this matchmaker stuff but also is expert in crafting forewords that fit the subject like O.J.'s glove. I've shared cover bylines with him before.

Thanks also to literary agent Rob Wilson, who also helped find a publisher for *Designated Hebrew*; to Rob Taylor, the University of Nebraska Press editor who believed in the story; and to Rob's talented colleague Courtney Ochsner.

Ronnie Joyner, the world's best baseball cartoonist, captured Al Clark so well that the old umpire actually bought the original artwork for his personal collection. Thanks, Ronnie, for continuing to grace my books with your brilliance.

Benjamin Bontekoe, a fellow Fair Lawn resident, did a masterful job of transcribing hours of interview tapes; and JetBlue, my favorite airline, provided vital round-trip tickets to Richmond, air gateway to Al Clark's adopted hometown of Williamsburg, Virginia. Thank yous and hugs go to Jenny Dervin and Sharon Jones of the airline's corporate communications department for cooperating not only on this project but on so many others.

I appreciate Ilene Dorf, one of my few remaining friends from snow-filled days at Syracuse University's Newhouse School, for her suggestions; Maryellen Nugent-Lee for securing photo reprint permissions; and the NMC Corporation for its counsel and guidance on yet another project.

I thank David Vincent of Retrosheet for allowing me to reprint Al Clark's year-by-year umpiring record plus a detailed listing of the sixty-five players, coaches, and managers he ejected. David, who doubles as official scorer of the Washington Nationals, is a cherished friend whom I see in the press box and at meetings of the Society for American Baseball Research. SABR stalwarts Vince Gennaro, Marc Appelbaum, and John Thorn have always been encouraging and helpful.

Thanks also go to Phyllis Deutsch, David Fenster, Allen Gross, Ed Lucas, Bob Nesoff, Sophie Nolan, Ken Olivenbaum, and other friends and family members who wanted the same piece of my time that my coauthor and editor demanded. I promise I will make it up to them.

And finally, thanks to Al Clark, who insisted from the get-go that he would be the easiest celebrity coauthor in my brief career as a ghostwriter. He was always affable, cooperative, and ready to work, even giving up his cherished golf game to talk into the tape recorder or telephone. I can't overlook his brothers Marty and Jeff, both of whom provided invaluable insights, and his longtime friends Red McGarry and Phil Moran. I even appreciate the racy messages Red sends me to start my day with a laugh.

DAN SCHLOSSBERG

Introduction

In twenty-six years as a Major League umpire, I never experienced anxiety. A lifetime of making controversial calls, arguing with angry managers, and receiving a constant barrage of boos, curses, and even thrown objects never bothered me.

Going to jail did.

As my wife and I pulled into the parking lot at the federal correctional facility in Petersburg, Virginia, I felt fear that I had never experienced before. More than anything else, it was a fear of the unknown. The pit in my stomach was eating at me from the inside, if that is at all physically possible. There was also an ache in my head that I had never felt before. My shoulders and my chest were shaking. The fear wouldn't abate until the car stopped and I was able to take some deep breaths. I was able to get out and start walking toward the administration doors of the facility. I remember vividly how terribly uncomfortable that feeling was.

Don't forget: I was in a foreign place and didn't know the language.

The minute I reported, they took away all my valuables. Although I was incarcerated, I was never behind bars, never in a cell. Not for a single day or a single hour. But my freedom was to be taken away for four months (120 days).

The most difficult thing about going to prison was knowing that I'd fucked up.

All the other stuff—the embarrassment over what I had lost—didn't matter. At that point, when I walked into the facility, all of that was insignificant. The peripheral stuff was not important.

What *was* important was the here and now. I had never been involved in any legal issue near that extent in my entire life and never thought that I would be in that kind of situation.

But, hey, stuff happens. *Shit* happens. You make the wrong decisions and you've got to pay for them. I made a mistake and had to pay for it. I created the situation myself, regardless of who else was involved. I had the wherewithal, always, to make the decision to say no. And for whatever reasons, I didn't. That created the situation that it did.

Years later I realized how ironic it was that I had been trained to make the correct decision—and make it quickly—but made the wrong decision when I had time to think about it.

Called Out but Safe

1 The Family Clark

I took a circuitous route to Major League Baseball.

My grandfather's family came to New York from Europe and went through the difficult immigration process at Ellis Island. They eventually owned a hotel on Far Rockaway, Long Island, called the Seaside House. That's where my grandfather met my grandmother.

Around 1920, when income tax came into existence, the family didn't want to raise any red flags with the government as far as their family-owned business was concerned, so they thought it would be best if they changed the family name. My grandfather graduated from college in New York with a degree in accounting; he became an accountant and changed his name from Sklarz to Clark. That's how my dad became Herbert Clark and I became Alan Clark. All our cousins on the paternal side are still named Sklarz.

My paternal grandfather was named Sidney and my grandmother was Sadie. My mother's parents were Phillip and Ida Marshall; from them I got my middle name. All four of them lived to hear me blow the shofar in my synagogue on the High Holy Days. I love the name Sidney. If I had been fortunate enough to have a daughter, she would have been named Sydney; Sydney Clark would have been a strong name for a woman.

I learned my love of baseball from my dad, Herb. He was a sportswriter so our afternoon conversations always had to do with sports. He took me to schoolboy games he was covering in and around Trenton, where we lived, and later to Major League games in New York and Philadelphia. Dad was a sportswriter in

Trenton, and he took me with him many times, to many places, including schoolyard ballparks. I loved it. When I was a kid of seven or eight years old I used to run around the bases while he was doing interviews. I think infield dirt got into my blood then.

Baseball was always my favorite sport and still is. I love the game of baseball. I remember Dad bought me *The Thinking Man's Guide to Baseball* when I was about twelve or thirteen years old. It was probably over my head at the time, and it seemed very complicated to me. But I got through it and still remember some of the formulas that the author, a New York sportswriter named Leonard Koppett, wrote. I actually met him years later and we talked about his book. But that was the genesis of my enjoyment of the game. As I got older, and got into baseball, I no longer was a baseball fan. A baseball fan likes teams and is a fan of teams and players. Instead I became a fan of baseball.

I think the game, no matter where it's played or how it's played, is such a thinking man's game, every day. Everything changes every day and every inning. So much depends upon the players and the situation—whether it's a left-handed pitcher or a right-handed pitcher, and so on. It's just a wonderful experience to go through an entire baseball game. And the game's strategy is so different if the score is 1–0 or 2–1, as opposed to 8–1 or 10–0. You look at the game differently. Your interest is different.

I am the oldest of three brothers who grew up in suburban Ewing Township, New Jersey, near the state capital of Trenton. I played high school baseball and basketball, but wasn't very good at either one. In basketball, I was a guard, a defensive ace, but I had white man's disease; I couldn't jump. I went wherever the ball went, while everybody else played a zone. I could run and worked hard. I played varsity basketball at Ewing, but don't think I've played a basketball game since.

I wasn't good enough to play baseball beyond high school. I tried to play later for the Eastern Kentucky University team but didn't make the cut. As a baseball player, I was a weak-hitting, weak-armed catcher, but always had good judgment; that's probably why I became an umpire. When people ask me why chose umping, I tell them that I realized it was a whole lot easier to *call* a curveball rather than to *hit* a curveball. I was probably a .280 hitter—not good enough to play anywhere.

At Ewing High School, I always blamed my coach for not playing me more. Like any player who didn't play, I just knew it wasn't my fault. But his evaluation was spot-on: as a catcher, I was probably a better umpire.

In the PAL Cub League I played for the Yankees team; one of my teammates was Bob Ryan, later a baseball writer, author, and ESPN talking head out of Boston. His first newspaper job was writing for my dad at the *Trenton Times*. One time during practice—Bob and I still laugh about this—he was pitching and beaned me, hitting me right in the head. He says that's the reason I became an umpire and he became a writer.

I learned about syllables when I was a young boy. My dad believed in spankings. The way I was disciplined and spanked helped me learn syllables. It was never child abuse—just good discipline. My dad would spank me on each syllable: "Do, you, un-der-stand?" That usually came after "You will al-ways o-bey your mother." That was a hard and harsh lesson.

My mother, on the other hand, was the most supportive mom there was. She was born in Massachusetts, came to Trenton, and met my dad at the Trenton Jewish Community Center. My parents were married more than fifty years and had a happy life, mostly in Trenton. Mother attended every baseball game I played. She followed my playing career and my umpiring career as she did my brother's careers. She was a great mom. She would protect us against my father. She would let things slide when we did things that were slightly wrong. She was a good mom, a loving mom. What more can I say than that?

I never had any intention of umpiring as a career. No one grows up wanting to be an umpire. You grow up wanting to be a player. But when that hard, harsh realization sets in that you're not good enough to be a player, you set your sights elsewhere.

I loved collecting baseball cards and wish I still had the ones I collected as a boy. I know one thing—the Mickey Mantle and Yogi Berra cards made great motorcycle sounds on my bicycle wheels. I cherished those cards, but never saw them again after I went to college. They may still be behind the upstairs eaves in the house where I grew up. I started umpiring in and around the Trenton area when I was sixteen, in part because it gave me an opportunity to earn extra money during summer vacations. As an amateur umpire, I was paid $6 per game (to work home plate) or $5.50 to work the bases. Out of that, I had to give 5 percent back to the assigner. I still hold the record in the Delaware Valley Umpires Association for working six hardball games in one day, earning a total of $36, minus 5 percent. That day, I called two Little League games, two Babe Ruth League games, an American Legion game, and a semi-pro game.

Even as an amateur, I wanted to be as good as I could be, at whatever level I was working. And who better to watch and to emulate than a Major League umpire? I knew Major League umpires were the best in the world.

As a student at Ewing High I was only average. I got by.

One of the things I remember most about high school is the work I had to do during the summer. I didn't think it was cool living through it, but I'll thank my dad until my last living breath for this: he made me read at least three books during the summer vacation—and then write reports on them. They didn't have to be sports books. They could be anything I chose. I had to read the book reports to him aloud while standing. I was constantly reading, all year, and learning how to write, too. I learned how to retain what I had read, put thoughts on paper, as in a book report, and did that every summer. Even senior year, the assignment stood. That's a memory I cherish.

Maybe that's why I turned to writing. Maybe that's why I wasn't afraid to speak in front of crowds. Maybe all that combined to put the pieces of the puzzle together so I could perform in public and not be intimidated. It all started when I was a kid. As my dad was assigning book reports, I realized that writing was fun. I still feel that with the correct adjectives and with a flair for words, you can draw a picture in one's mind as they're reading. The whole concept intrigued me.

I also learned to type, thanks to my dad. When I was a sophomore in high school we had two elective classes to choose. My dad made me elect typing. I was the only guy in the class. It was embarrassing at the time but it turned out quite well, because my social life got a whole lot better. And I learned how to type. I became a good typist and have used that ability for my whole life. While in college, where reports had to be typed, I charged fifty to seventy-five cents a page to type other guys' reports.

When I was growing up my best friend was my next-door neighbor, Phil Moran. Our doors were twenty-nine feet apart—we measured the distance. We owned many pets—parakeets, dogs, rabbits—together, fed them together, and buried them together.

Phil was Roman Catholic but knew my haftorah better than I did. We had a vinyl record that my rabbi, Solomon Pole, had gotten with a recording of the haftorah in Hebrew. I played it over and over and over. Since Flip (my nickname for him) was always in our house, we would chant and sing it together. I would say, "Flip, it's your turn," and he would say, "Al, it's your turn." That's how we learned it. At the ceremony, he chanted the haftorah with me. He also lip-synched my speech to the congregation. I'm the guy who went to Hebrew School. It was one of the many things we did together.

Flip and I were in "business" together, from selling lemonade to shoveling snow and cutting grass. We put up a basketball hoop in his backyard. He said to put the bricks as a stabilizer in front of the pole that held up the backboard but I said to put them in the back. We did what he said and the backboard came out crooked. To this day, I blame him for making it crooked.

He was always the smart guy—he went to Canisius College and Rutgers University Law School Camden, and eventually became a lawyer. I attended Eastern Kentucky and became an umpire.

One of my best childhood memories is going to my first big league game. I was a little boy, about seven or eight, when my dad took me to Yankee Stadium. The Yankees weren't very good then but I was very excited. Here I was, a young Yankees fan, going to Yankee Stadium for the first time. It was just like Billy Crystal said: walking through the portals and seeing all that the green grass was mesmerizing.

The Red Sox were there. Both Mickey Mantle and Ted Williams were playing. We sat along the first base side, way upstairs. There were a lot of empty seats that day. As the game progressed I was looking at the players, I was looking at the field, I was watching the game, and, all of a sudden, I turned to my left and saw my dad with his legs over the seats in front of him. To my amazement, he was sleeping. Years later, it occurred to me how ironic it was that my dad fell asleep at Yankee Stadium. Although I didn't sleep that day, many people later accused me of sleeping when I was working behind the plate at Yankee Stadium.

My dad was a writer but he was biased. He covered the New York Yankees, and he was a Yankees fan. Whatever the Yanks did was absolutely fine with him. If something went against the Yankees, he would write that the Yankees got screwed. The team certainly appreciated him; Gil McDougald once gave my dad a pair of his shoes. Herb had them resoled and wore them for years. He proudly said he was wearing Yankee shoes.

My dad's passion for the team and my career as an umpire later caused a conflict for us both one night. My dad was covering a game I was working at Yankee Stadium. There was a controversial play that I called against the home team. He was asked to go into the umpires' dressing room as the pool reporter. All the writers knew I was his son. He came in and was welcomed by all the umpires. They all knew Herb and liked him—but on that particular day, he asked me a slanted, pointed question that implied I blew a play against the Yankees. He wanted to know if I was in the right position to make the call. At that point I wasn't Al Clark, Herb's son; I was Al Clark, the umpire. I took offense and not so politely asked him to leave the room.

I was still living in New Jersey and in the heat of the moment had forgotten I had ridden with him from Trenton to Yankee Stadium. After he was ejected, I realized I had to meet him in the working press room, where he was writing and filing his story. Needless to say, that trip back to Trenton was a long ride for Al, the son. I was lectured about decorum, about how to treat dads. I tried to explain that at that point he wasn't my dad but just a writer being biased and stupid. He didn't quite see it that way.

I was glad to get back to Trenton that night. I drove myself to the ballpark the next day.

Things were simpler when I was growing up.

As a patrol boy in elementary school, we used to go on field trips. The Phillies had Patrol Boy Day on a Saturday in May that attracted busloads of kids. The stands of Connie Mack Stadium were filled with patrol boys from all over the Delaware Valley.

Even though Trenton was closer to Philadelphia, I became a Yankees fan because my dad was a Yankees fan. Yankee Stadium was where we went. As I got a bit older, I used to take the train into Philadelphia, to old Connie Mack Stadium in North Philly, and that was a good time, a good experience, and everything, but I was still a fan of the Yankees.

Unlike friends whose boyhood heroes were Mickey Mantle or Roger Maris, my idol was a left-handed pitcher from Trenton named Al Downing. Although I'm eight or ten years younger, I knew him a little bit as a youngster. After he signed with the Yankees I wrote to him as any youngster might in those days. A true professional, he always wrote me back.

When Downing got to the big leagues he wore number 24 for the Yankees. From that point I tried to wear number 24 wherever I played. When I first got to the big leagues American League umpires didn't wear numbers. Years into my career AL officials opted to number their umpires. We were given the opportunity to choose numbers according to seniority. I chose number 24 and wore it for all the years I remained in the big leagues.

Downing wore 24 only with the Yankees. He went on to Los Angeles before finishing his career with Cincinnati. He also spent time with the Oakland A's and Milwaukee Brewers. That didn't make any difference to me. I kept a scrapbook on him when I was a kid and followed his career. I wanted to be just like Al Downing.

He reached the big leagues before I did and is remembered today as the pitcher who gave up a grand slam to Ken Boyer in the 1964 World Series and Hank Aaron's 715th home run—the one that made him the career home run champion—ten years later. He also led the American League in strikeouts in 1964.

Steve Braun, a friendly rival, made it to the Major Leagues, too. He played for Minnesota, Kansas City, Seattle, and St. Louis. We grew up together and were about the same age. Steve was from Hopewell Township, a suburb of Princeton. I don't know that I rooted for him so much as I hoped he did well. I played against him in both baseball and basketball while in high school.

One of the best high school basketball players in New Jersey, Steve averaged 28 or 29 points per game. He was a little taller than I was but also stronger and a better athlete. When we were going to play Hopewell Valley, my high school basketball coach decided to employ a box-and-one on defense with me as the chaser. I was to chase Steve Braun all night. I had a very good night, holding him to about 12 or 13 points before fouling out. That one game might have been the shining moment of my entire high school basketball career.

Years later, when Steve was playing and I was umpiring in the Venezuelan Winter League, he and his wife celebrated Thanksgiving with my wife, Karen, and me in our apartment in Caracas.

My life also had some unexpected twists and turns.

Before I broke into umpiring as a profession, I was a substitute teacher in a vocational/technical high school and other high schools. It wasn't fulfilling for me to be a teacher. I wanted to do something else, and that's when I turned to writing. I was primarily a sportswriter for newspapers in Trenton but I also did some feature writing for magazines. I had been a feature writer for the *Eastern Progress*, the newspaper at Eastern Kentucky University, and enjoyed the interaction with athletes and others in the college community and then having a byline in the paper.

I'm the eldest of three siblings. Marty is ten years younger than I am and Jeffrey is seven years younger. Marty lives in Lawrenceville, outside Trenton, and Jeffrey lives in Chandler, near Phoenix. Jeff loved sports but wasn't the athlete Marty and I were. Marty even followed my lead and was a catcher when he played baseball. In our house, growing up in a sports environment with my dad, you either loved sports or were a great student. Jeff was the great student.

I love my brothers very much. I used to take both of them with me everywhere. I would take Jeff and his best friend, Ricky Meadow, to see the New York Giants and Philadelphia Eagles at Palmer Stadium in Princeton on the university campus. That was an exhibition game that they looked forward to every year. We used to sit in the top row, the top seats, somewhere in the stadium. But you know what? It didn't make any difference: we were at the stadium and it was a great day with my brother and his friend. We always had a great time.

I had a big newspaper boy's basket on my bike, and I used to put Marty in the basket. We traveled to watch baseball games, to play baseball, to the store—wherever—and he loved it.

Jeff used to have a little trouble with possessives. Our grandparents lived in Miami, and every December, we would pack the car and go to Miami with mom and dad. I talked about going to Miami from Thanksgiving on. Jeff could never quite get "Miami." He always called it "Yourami."

Even though I followed my father's career footsteps for a while, our family took different career paths. There was a time, however, that my brother Marty thought about becoming a professional umpire.

Long after his aspirations dissipated, we actually worked a game together. While barnstorming at the end of spring training one year, the Baltimore Orioles hosted the St. Louis Cardinals in an exhibition game at old RFK Stadium in Washington. Since there were only three umpires assigned, I called Marty Springstead, supervisor of AL umps, and asked if my brother Marty, an amateur umpire, could join me on the field and umpire third base. I had been assigned to work home plate and promised to take care of my brother if anything out of the ordinary occurred during the game. It was a pleasure to walk onto a big league field with my brother and umpire a game together.

Cal Ripken Sr. came out to exchange the lineup card for the Orioles. I introduced him to my brother. Cal, in his inimitable way, said something a little derogatory. Cal Sr. didn't have a whole lot of nice things to say to any umpires. He said he felt sorry for Marty being my brother and having to put up with a big league umpire in the family.

It was an inconsequential spring training game but created a great memory for the Clark family. It was the only time we umpired together.

Marty became an umpire in the Delaware Valley Umpires Association and was president of the association. He is a New Jersey state scholastic rules interpreter. He also officiates basketball and soccer. Marty has earned much respect as an official and I am very proud of him.

Although he might have liked to join me in the Major Leagues, it's really difficult to follow an older brother's footsteps in the same profession, especially a public one like professional sports. Marty had aspirations to become an NBA referee. He got as far as sessions with the Philadelphia 76ers and New York Knicks in their preseason camps. The Celtics also flew him up to Boston for a session.

Long after we were adults and had families of our own, Marty and I had a falling out, a rift that kept us apart for twenty years. It took some maturity and understanding but we were able to put everything behind us and become the brothers that we should be. We may have even grown closer.

We were all in Phoenix for my dad's funeral in 2008 when my sister-in-law Kathy, Jeff's wife, sat us down: Jeffrey, Marty, and me. She said, "The fight between you two guys was something that neither your mother nor your father appreciated, liked, or could understand." She looked at me and said, "Do you want to have Marty in your life as your brother?" I said, "Yes." She looked at Marty and said, "Do you want to have Alan in your life as your brother?" He said, "Yes."

Then she said, "This is what is going to happen: from this point forward, neither of you will ever talk to each other again about the feud you had that lasted all these years. From now on, you guys will only be brothers. You'll care about each other as brothers do, you'll love each other as brothers do, and you'll accept that whatever happened in the past makes no difference at all. Nobody was right and nobody was wrong. It was just lost time."

I truly regret losing all those years because Marty's sons are really into baseball. Even though they missed going on the road and spending time with me, it was my loss. I love those kids very much and I could have been the best Uncle Al in the world. But the stupid feud between Marty and me stood in the way.

I'm not even sure how the whole argument started. We can talk about each of us being stubborn, not accepting what the other was saying. Maybe I didn't do enough for Marty to facilitate a situation for him to get into the big leagues as an official, either the NBA or organized baseball.

Marty became one of the best schoolboy officials in the state of New Jersey and is very happy. He and wife, Marie, and his sons are a magnificent family and he's a great father. He may not have managed that had he gone on the road. That's why I chose not to have any kids of my own; I didn't think I could give them the time they deserved.

Because I never had any children of my own, my five nephews have been a big part of my life. Marty and Marie have two sons, Kyle and Casey; Jeff and his wife, Kathy, have three sons, Kevin, Michael, and Tyler Jacob (TJ)—and two granddaughters, Katelyn and Keagan.

We have a very close-knit family. We are totally into each other's lives. The miles that separate us don't mean a whole lot. We chat often and stay close with each other, as families should.

2 Getting Started

I left Ewing Township for college but wasn't sure what I would study and certainly did not know what I would do to earn a living. I liked sports but wasn't good enough to play baseball or basketball professionally. I also liked writing about sports, as my dad did. I liked umpiring, even though my only experience had been as an amateur.

Going from central New Jersey to Eastern Kentucky University was a huge culture shock, but I had a friend who made my first away-from-home experience much easier. I became friendly with EKU's head basketball coach, Guy Strong. He played a very substantial role in my life before baseball. Strong played on Adolph Rupp's early 1950s national championship teams, became a high school teacher and guidance counselor in Louisville, and went to Eastern Kentucky as head basketball coach, then to Oklahoma State as basketball coach, and finally to George Rogers Clark High School in Winchester, Kentucky, as head basketball coach and guidance counselor.

I was a writer on the *Eastern Progress* college newspaper, covering EKU football and basketball. I went on road trips with the basketball team. I got to spend a lot of time with the coach. We had a great relationship. He would allow me to spend hours in his office, sometimes until two or three o'clock in the morning after games. We not only rehashed the games and why they were won or lost, but also the why(s) of life, the getting along, the not getting along, the not taking any shit from anybody, the understanding and realization that other people always have an agenda. He taught it was my responsibility to figure it out and deal with it, whatever it was, and to stay as positive as possible.

Among the many things Guy Strong taught me were diligence, efficiency, and keeping things in order. He also taught me proficiency; you couldn't be successful without being proficient. He was very influential in my young adult formative years. He's in his eighties now and we still stay in touch. I have as much respect for him as I have for anybody I've ever met anywhere.

I actually had two different stints at Eastern Kentucky. The first one started in 1966 after I graduated from high school. I flunked out in 1968, went home, and attended Mercer County Community College to pass the courses I had failed.

I reapplied to EKU and was accepted in 1969 but left after that year with the understanding that I would be the public relations director for the Pittsburgh Condors in the American Basketball Association. I interviewed with Condors GM Marty Blake. Initially Blake thought I'd be a good fit for his young organization but later changed his mind. He cited my lack of experience for such an assignment.

Back in Trenton again, I was a substitute teacher at East Brunswick Vo-tech High School and a few other schools. I wrote for the *Trentonian* newspaper, but after living with a sportswriter for all my formative years, I decided I wanted to eat steaks rather than hamburgers the rest of my life. In order to do that, I was not going to be a writer in Trenton, New Jersey.

So I thought again about umpiring. I asked Bus Saidt, the national baseball writer for the *Trenton Times*, if he could investigate how to get into organized baseball as an umpire. He did and I applied successfully to umpire school.

I had learned the names of a few respected older umpires, guys like Bill Haller, Nestor Chylak, John Kibler, Ed Vargo, and Larry Napp. Those were guys I aspired to be like—and would later get to know, and, in some cases, work with. They were so prideful and they relayed that pride to me years later when I was a young professional umpire.

When I attended the umpire specialization course in 1972, Major League Baseball still subsidized the umpire school. There were only two schools for umpires: the specialization course and the Al Somers School, which later became the Harry Wendelstedt School. My program was based in St. Petersburg, Florida, and lasted five weeks. It was run by the director of Minor League operations for Major League Baseball, Barney Deary.

Acceptance was more stringent then. Baseball could pick and choose their students. There were height, sight restrictions, weight, and other physical requirements. That is not the case anymore. Today's umpire schools accept all applicants. Back then, 250 people applied, 150 were accepted, and 22 of us eventually earned jobs in the Minor Leagues. That was the most productive class to date, too. Six of us eventually became either American or National League staff members. Among my classmates, Eddie Montague and I were the first from that class to make the Majors. Then with expansion, Durwood Merrill, Steve Palermo, Mike Reilly, and Vic Voltaggio landed MLB appointments.

When the course started, I was pretty confident. Like everybody else there, I thought I knew the rulebook. But a little knowledge is a dangerous thing; the more I learned about the rules, the more I realized I didn't know a damn thing. I was like most players and most managers today—they have no idea about the intricacies of the rulebook.

Everybody knows three strikes and you're out, right? But that's not always the case. Maybe the catcher drops the ball on the third strike and first base is unoccupied. Then it's not three strikes and you're out, and the catcher throws the ball to first base or tags the runner. Is a batter or runner out if the bases are loaded, the catcher drops the ball, and he doesn't tag the batter/runner or throw to first base to retire the batter/runner? No. But what else can the catcher do? He can touch home plate, because the bases are loaded and the runner is forced. There are so many nuances to the rules—like the difference between obstruction and interference. Little things like where do umpires look and how do they rotate? And why?

There are *three* teams on the field every day. The third team is the crew of umpires. They communicate with each other. They talk with each other. They have signals just like a third base coach does. And all that is for the coordination of their teamwork. When you see a player sliding into third base, sometimes it's the third base umpire that makes the call. Sometimes it's the second-base umpire at third base. And sometimes it's the home-plate umpire, if he comes up the baseline. It all depends on how many guys are on base, how many outs there are, where the ball was hit, how the crew rotates.

That all is known before the ball is hit because umpires communicate with each other to coordinate their movements. When I talk to groups I tell them the next time they see a big league ball game, they should take a half inning and watch the umpires instead of the players. Especially if it's not a 1-2-3 inning. Watch how the umpires position themselves. Watch how the first base umpire with nobody on base will position himself back on the outfield grass, and then as soon as somebody gets on base, he'll come to a position behind first base and in foul territory. See how the second base umpire will go from the outfield to the infield. Watch where he positions himself on the shortstop side or the first base side of second base. And watch what happens when the ball is hit and where everybody moves. The precision of the umpires' movements on the field is almost like that of a ballet.

Fans are amazed when they understand better what's happening with the umpires on the field. I've had people come back and tell me that my half-hour talk about the umpires enhanced their enjoyment of watching baseball games. It has enhanced their enjoyment because suddenly there was so much more to see other than the pitcher throwing the ball, the hitter hitting, and the outfielders or infielders fielding and throwing. And that's something that makes baseball the greatest game in the world.

Thanks to the umpire schools, umpires became younger and more proficient. Someone who exemplified that proficiency was the highly educated University of Texas graduate Jim Evans. One of the youngest umpires ever to reach the big leagues, he was only twenty-two when he joined the American League staff in 1971.

I had the pleasure of working with Evans for a number of years. We used to have great rules discussions in the dressing room and on flights between games. Jim shared his knowledge of the rules and the rulebook with anybody with whom he partnered. He loved researching the history of baseball's rules, and eventually wrote a book on baseball rules in all situations. His school produced some very good umpires; anybody who graduated was rich in the knowledge of the rules and their interpretation. Jimmy thought to understand a rule fully, you had to understand why the rule was there in the first place.

I did not get a job out of school. I was first assigned to the Atlanta Braves spring training complex in West Palm Beach, Florida, and then was to go home until the middle of June when the short-season Class A leagues were scheduled to begin. I was slated to umpire in the New York–Penn League my first year. But someone dropped out of the Midwest League about two weeks into the season, and that's when Barney Deary called and asked me to go to Burlington, Iowa, and start my Minor League career there.

I hardly knew where Iowa was, let alone *Burlington*, Iowa. I was a good little Jewish kid from Trenton, New Jersey, and my first partner was a nineteen-year-old youngster named Wes "Smokey" Trietel. He was from the Cincinnati area and spoke with a lisp; he ended up being a scab during a labor dispute years later. I was a college-educated guy who was much more mature than my partner. I felt like a babysitter.

When we were in Danville, Illinois, I was working home plate. There was a lady right behind me, screaming and yelling at any movement I made. She just kept it up continuously. Finally, she yelled, "Hey, ump! Hey, ump!" I turned around and acknowledged her. She said, "If you went on *What's My Line* [an old TV quiz show] and had all of your home plate equipment on, the panel *still* wouldn't guess your occupation." I just had to laugh.

Jim Doster, the president of the Midwest League, had his office in Decatur, Illinois. During the summer, he traveled extensively to the league's cities. I met him for the first time in Quincy, Illinois, sometime in June. He invited me to breakfast one morning. I had been in his league for just a couple of months. He had retired from business and was a grandfatherly individual. During our breakfast, he told me he'd been the Midwest League president for ten years and enjoyed his association with the Minor Leagues very much. He also indicated I would probably be assigned to work the league's playoffs that September. Then I probably would not be back in his league the following year. He indicated I would certainly be moving to Double-A in 1973. That made me very happy and gave me incentive to work that much harder for the rest of the '72 Midwest League season. When the Midwest League season finally ended, I was selected to work the league playoffs. I was then invited to the Florida Instructional League, an acceleration program for both young players and umpires trying to get to the Majors. That lasted until just before Thanksgiving.

The next year, I was promoted to the Texas League and invited back to the Florida Instructional League. In the middle of the FIL schedule, someone quit in Venezuela and Deary asked me to take his place. It was unheard of at the time for a second-year umpire to leave the country and go to the Caribbean. Deary must have seen some potential in me.

How could I say no? I knew that experience represented a fast track to the Majors. The carrot at the end of the stick was the big leagues. I certainly did not want to be a career Minor League umpire. Any umpire would do anything to enhance his goal of reaching the big leagues. I went to Venezuela in my second winter of organized baseball.

I didn't come back to the United States until after the winter league playoffs in January. I took the month of February off before heading back to Florida for spring training. After only two years working in a Minor League spring training camp, I was invited to my first American League spring training and assigned to the Orlando area. Obviously quite happy about that, I couldn't wait to get started and work my first Major League spring training game.

While in Venezuela I learned I had once again been promoted for the regular season. My Minor League contract was purchased by the Triple-A American Association. The president there was Joe Ryan, another very good Minor League administrator. I enjoyed working for Ryan for two years. I was assigned to work his league playoffs both years I was there.

The Triple-A ballparks were small then, and the fans were more intimate with the umpires and the players. We were in Wichita, Kansas, where the ballpark was an old, rickety, wooden structure. My partner had home plate and I was working at first base. There was an old leather-lunged guy in the stands behind home plate. He was unmerciful toward umpires every day. He really gave my partner a tongue lashing.

I rotated to home plate the next day and couldn't wait to get there. The old fellow was there again and for three innings yelled disparaging remarks at me. He was just being a real pain, a real thorn in our side. After the third inning, between innings, I went back to the screen.

Very respectfully, I said, "Sir, you're pretty tough today." He said, "You betcha. If you were any kind of umpire, you wouldn't make those calls." I said, "Were you here last night?" He said, "You betcha I was here last night and that guy last night did a terrible job." I said, "Lemme ask you a question. Is that your wife with you today?" He said, "Yeah, that's my wife, what of it?" Then I said, loudly enough for her to hear, "That woman you had with you last night was a whole lot better looking than your wife." The guy suddenly went silent. We didn't hear him the next half inning. I looked back to see what happened. He was gone, never to be seen or heard from again.

Oklahoma City was also in the American Association. One day, while I was having lunch with my partner Ted Hendry, we heard sirens. Ted was from Oregon and I was from New Jersey. What the hell did we know about tornado sirens? We looked at each other, looked for emergency vehicles, and didn't see anything. All of a sudden, the wind started swirling and blowing hard. And it got dark. We went back into the restaurant and asked, "What's going on?" They looked at us like we had three heads. Having never seen a tornado, except in pictures, we did the most intelligent thing we could do: we went out to look at it. We saw the funnel and we saw it waving, just like in *The Wizard of Oz*. It wasn't close enough to pick us up but it was quite a sight. It was like experiencing an earthquake for the first time, as I would later find out. Once the storm passed, everything was fine. Noah was right: the rain has got to stop sometime. You don't screw with Mother Nature. And don't think you can beat her.

Hendry and I ate a lot of meals together during our Minor League days. One morning, we were in Shreveport, Louisiana, having breakfast at a little diner. We had an eighteen-year-old waitress who didn't know anything about Jewish people or Kosher food. She sauntered over and asked delicately and nicely in her southern drawl if she could take our order. I asked for a couple of eggs over medium and some bacon and rye toast. I asked if I could have the bacon crisp. She said yes, and as she was turning, I said, "Oh, one more thing." She said, "Yes, sir?" I said, "Is that bacon kosher?" She looked at me, tilted her head, and said, "I don't know, sir, but I'll find out." This by itself is funny because bacon cannot be kosher. She walked away, came back a couple of minutes later, and said in all seriousness, "Excuse me, sir, that bacon is not kosher—it's Oscar Mayer."

Our travels through the American Association took us through St. Louis one day. The Cardinals were home and one of the National League umpires assigned to the game was Harry Wendelstedt. We got to Busch Stadium early and called down to the umpires' dressing room. Wendelstedt had gotten there early, too, but the rest of his crew had not arrived. He invited us to join him. Harry couldn't have been more gracious and classy to two Minor League umpires just passing through. I'll never forget how big league he was to us.

John Kibler, the longtime National League umpire, was also especially nice to me when I was just starting. What a gentleman he was. I was not only proud to know him but also proud that we shared the same birthdate, January 9. He gave me the first umpire travel case I ever owned.

My generation of umpires learned a lot from the previous generation. We didn't know it at the time, but what we were absorbing we would later give to the young umpires who came up after we were established in the Major Leagues.

There were so many guys whom I hope I mentored correctly— umpires like Jim Joyce, Dale Scott, Brian O'Nora, Mark Wegner, and others who are middle and senior umpires now. They're all good young umpires who have ten or more years in the big leagues. When they were promoted, I had between fifteen and twenty-five years. I would give them the same benefit of my experience that guys like Bill Haller and Larry McCoy gave me. They helped form the attitudes that I carried throughout my career. I hope some of those attitudes are being employed by those I mentored. If they are, I am certainly proud of them.

After the end of the 1974 season, I traveled back to Venezuela for another year. I had signed a contract the previous winter to go back. I learned that in Venezuela, when thirty thousand people yell, "Kill the umpire!" they almost mean it. In the little town of Valencia, they had a Brylcream rubber ball day. I'll never forget it. They had about thirty thousand people in the ballpark on a Saturday. I made a call at home plate that went against the Valencia club. The club had made a mistake by giving out those rubber balls before the game. All of a sudden, thirty thousand rubber balls came out of the stands aimed at me. It took an hour and a half to clear the field of all the balls. Now this was great marketing. They then had *another* rubber ball game the next weekend. The club gave them out all over again. That time, the balls weren't distributed to the fans until *after* the game, as they were on their way out of the stadium.

Spring training 1976 was my second American League spring training invitation. All the Minor League umpires who were invited to Major League spring training knew there were open spots on the umpire roster. There were five Minor League umpires vying for two AL spots.

Near the end of spring training AL supervisor of umpires Dick Butler invited Greg Kosc, out of Pacific Coast League, and me to have dinner with him at a restaurant named the Buccaneer on Longboat Key outside Sarasota, Florida. Both Greg and I were hoping and suspecting we had been selected to be promoted into the American League as full-fledged staff members. However, as much as we suspected, nothing was certain. We just weren't sure.

Greg was there with his wife, Charlene. I was there solo. It wasn't until after dinner that Butler said anything about why we were there. He just kept us hanging. How could we enjoy the dinner with the anticipation of the rest of our lives hanging in the balance? Finally, over dessert and coffee, Butler congratulated us both on being selected to join the American League staff. Greg was to open the season with future Hall of Fame umpire Nestor Chylak and I was to join Bill Haller's crew, which consisted of McCoy and Ron Luciano. I was going to Arlington, Texas, where the Rangers were hosting the Minnesota Twins on Opening Day

1976. There is certainly something special about all opening days. However, when it's your first as a Major League umpire, you just never forget it.

That was the culmination of a lot of hard work and sacrifice. It was the fulfillment of a dream that was and still is paramount in my life. Signing that first big league contract is one of those life-changing moments. I'm sure it's the same for a player, coach, manager, or anybody who reaches for the ultimate and makes it. It's the same for an author signing his first big contract. It's a big deal. The feeling stays with you for the rest of your life.

3 The Art of Umpiring

It's virtually impossible to find people able to make consequential snap decisions without a meeting, without a conference, without going to committee—and who have to be right 99.5 percent of the time. Yet that's the scrutiny all umpires undergo *before* they get to the Major Leagues.

Umpires have to deal with players in the big leagues who are the best in the world. The hand-eye coordination they possess is a God-given talent. Umpires are trained to judge whether those skills are applied successfully in any given situation.

Umpire training is rigorous; they are judged not only for their ability to call balls and strikes, fairs and fouls, safes and outs; but also how they handle situations, apply the rule book, and interpret different rules in different circumstances and situations. Those are all things that make big league umpires as good as they are.

Being an umpire takes poise, maturity, psychology, mastery of body language, and an ability to maintain composure when everyone around them has lost theirs. Umpires have to know how to control fights. What do they do when twenty-five guys are charging from one side of the field and twenty-five guys are coming from the other side of the field and nobody's willing to listen? How do they handle that and still have control?

If you're an umpire and you're experienced, you know the answer. When you break that concentration, the intensity all professional players possess, they regain some of their composure. As soon as they do, you've won the argument. They're not going to go back to that level of intensity again.

Administrators in baseball think of umpires as necessary evils. They don't care about us until five minutes before a game. If we don't show up on the field, they think, "Hey, where the hell are the umpires?" And that's the first time they think of us.

We realize it's an anonymous job. I don't have any issue with that. No umpire takes issue with that. We're not the stars; we're not the people. We're on the periphery of celebrity, and I believe that we are an important part of the game—an integral part of the game—but we are not the game. We are highly trained professionals, the best in the world at what we do.

Just because an umpire hasn't got the experience, hasn't got name recognition, or makes a questionable call doesn't mean he's a bad umpire. Umpires in the big leagues are fantastic people of judgment. They know what they're doing out there. Seldom is a mistake made by an umpire. Seldom will you see a play at a base when an umpire is not there. If it's at second base, it may not be the second base umpire. It might be the third base umpire. It might even be the first base umpire. But one of them will get there.

If an umpire is in the big leagues, he's the best in the world. He's been taught, trained, and scrutinized. He's gone through the Minor League trials and tribulations of getting to the big leagues.

The umpires are the third team on the field on any given day. The Yankees might be playing the Tigers. But the third team would be Rick Reed's crew, Joe Brinkman's crew, or Tim McClelland's crew. The four umpires communicate with each other in sign language. We talk with each other between innings. We make each other aware of situations as simple as infield flies or timed plays with two outs—just so everybody is on the same page. As my crew chief, Reed always insisted there should be four eyes on the ball at all times. He didn't care which four eyes, but four eyes had to be on the ball. Preventive umpiring—being aware of what's going on around you before it happens—keeps everybody alert. When a discrepancy occurs on the field and umpires huddle, the main objective is to get the play correct, whether it is a rule interpretation or a judgment decision that is changeable.

In my twenty-six years of service, one day stands as the most difficult I had as a home plate umpire calling balls and strikes.

It was a very hot, humid summer day in Chicago's old Comiskey Park. Wilbur Wood, a left-handed knuckleball pitcher, was pitching for the White Sox against the Angels' Nolan Ryan, a young pitcher who threw very hard. Two more different pitchers never faced each other in a Major League game. The knuckleball would flutter to the plate at 67 miles per hour; Ryan's fastball would register almost 102. Wood lasted six innings and Ryan pitched seven. This young umpire was never happier to see two starting pitchers relieved.

Most of the players in the big leagues are really good guys. They understand, and they're mature enough to realize, that they worked hard to get to the big leagues, but so did the umpires.

I earned a decent reputation. The old guys would tell the younger guys that Clark is a good, fair umpire. If you let him do his job, he'll let you do your job. But if you fuck with him, he will fuck with you. That's a great reputation to have as an umpire. I consider that assessment fair.

There's a memorabilia collector in the Williamsburg area who went to see Steve Garvey when he was signing autographs at an autograph signing session. The collector asked Garvey, "Hey, Steve. We have a mutual friend. Remember Al Clark, the umpire?" And Garvey said, "Yeah, of course I remember Al. We were in the All-Star Game together in San Francisco." He said, "What did you think of him?" And Garvey said, "He was a real fair guy." As an umpire, I couldn't ask for anything more.

I did not model myself after any other umpire; I took things from different umpires and incorporated what worked best for me. For instance, there was nothing about Ron Luciano anyone would want to emulate on the field but there was a lot from Bill

Haller to incorporate into your persona on the field. Other guys also.

Ideally, an umpire wants to create a recognizable personality all his own—to develop an individual style that is unique. Was there ever a doubt who was umpiring when Dutch Rennert was calling balls and strikes? Or how about Bill Haller, with his right arm bent at the elbow, punching the air in front of his outside chest protector? I believe that personality added to the fan experience. But it does not exist very much today.

I admired Lee Weyer, who controlled a game as well as anybody in the National League; the calmness of Rick Reed; and the rules knowledge of Jim Evans, who even wrote a cross-reference to the rulebook called the *Major League Baseball Rules Index*. Working with Evans made umpires better because his crew always talked about the rules and rule interpretations. It was uncanny how often a subject just discussed by that crew would come up during a game. I worked with Jimmy a lot of years and I learned to more appreciate the rules than I did before. It was always fun for umpires to talk and argue rules and situations.

It's fun to create your own personality. When I see somebody outside the ballpark and I tell them I'm a Major League umpire, they ask, "Which one?" I say, "I call strikes this way." If they know the game, they say, "Oh, my God, you're him!" That's fun and I think it adds to our game.

I earned a reputation for being a pitcher's umpire. I believed that if it was a hittable pitch, it probably should be called a strike at the Major League level. That's the way I defined it, certainly within the parameters of home plate and the defined strike zone. The strike zone is defined in the rulebook as the area under the armpits to the top of the knees in a player's hitting position. But the hitting position is different from a batting stance. Rickey Henderson stood in a severe crouch. If he took a pitch and an umpire called a strike around his neck, it was because of his batting stance. When he actually hit, he would come out of that crouched position and he'd have a much larger strike zone. Umpires called the strike zone from his hitting position, not his batting stance.

But I also believe that it takes trained umpires to call strikes and outs. Anybody can stand out there and call balls and safes.

Tough calls come with the job. Controversies come with the uniform. We don't even think about them. We handle them. Isn't that exactly what you would want if you were a participant, if you were a club official, or if you were a league official? Wouldn't you want your game officials to have no investment in the game whatsoever? Despite the arguments, the tough calls, the tough situations, we'll handle them. There isn't an umpire out there on the big league field who's afraid to make a tough call. Why not? We don't think about it. We just do it. We report what we see. Nothing is premeditated. And I don't want to work with a guy if anything he does *is* premeditated.

BRAWLS

I ejected about seventy people in my career, which is about average for someone who lasted twenty-six years in the Majors.

Base brawls occur when both team's benches and bullpens empty and rush toward each other. Fortunately no one is usually injured during these brouhahas. There's a lot of pushing, shoving, and shouting—but few fisticuffs. One reason for that is the umpires are good at handling them. First they will try to stop the combatants before actual engagement occurs. If that doesn't work, the umps stay out of the way until the first wave of aggression subsides. Only then is action taken. The umpires will direct the teams to separate and go back to their respective dugouts and bullpens. They expect the managers and coaches to help. As the players separate, the umpires try to divert their attention away from the opposing teams and from themselves. The hope is that tempers have cooled by that point and players will pay attention. Then the game can continue without further incident.

Rivalries are great for the game, and they can often lead to brawls. Although the Giants and Dodgers had a fierce one when both played in New York, the friction between the New York Yankees and Boston Red Sox remains white hot. It could have something to do with the crossover of their fan base or the rivalries of the two cities. Whatever the reason, those fans love their teams with great passion.

That passion exploded during a 1999 game I worked at Fenway Park during the American League Championship Series. Tim Tschida, the second base umpire, had called a Sox player out but the fans disagreed and showed their displeasure by littering the field with debris. Working behind home plate, I stopped play and ordered the Yankees to their dugout until the field could be cleared and the fans could be brought under control. Ballpark security and Boston police did a great job. Order was restored and the game resumed within ten minutes.

After the game, I retired to a little restaurant next to the hotel where I was staying. I was watching the recap on TV with my wife and some friends. The Boston announcers were saying the umpires pulled the Yankees off the field, and the fans were so irate that they were not letting the umpires out of Fenway Park. I was sitting in a restaurant a long way from Fenway Park. All six umpires and their families and guests departed the ballpark together an hour earlier. The talking heads were 100 percent wrong. A whole lot of people said, "Al, what are you doing here?" I said the people doing the talking on television know not what they're speaking of. Their opinions are valueless. They never do their homework. How many reporters or talking heads come into an umpires' dressing room to find out what actually happened in an argument or a situation?

Neither Boston nor New York has a monopoly on rowdy fans. They can appear on any given day with any given team. We never worried about the fans in the stands, but it was always scary when a fan jumped the fence and headed straight toward an umpire. We didn't know whether that fan wanted to shake a hand or pull a knife.

Fights can happen anywhere, at any time—and can involve athletes most fans would consider least likely to brawl. Consider the famous altercation between Nolan Ryan and Robin Ventura a few years ago. Ryan, who is now retired as the president of the Texas Rangers, and Ventura, now the manager of the Chicago White Sox, were both intense competitors. When pitching, Nolan wouldn't yield an inch. Robin was more quiet, but was a guy who would never let up. Robin thought he got hit intentionally and didn't care who was on the mound. He was going to let that pitcher know he couldn't do that. The joke is that was the only time in Nolan's career that he got five hits in one game. Those kinds of things happen and are part of the game because you're dealing with 99.5 percent Type A personalities—people who are used to working hard and achieving success.

Umpires are Type A people too. Otherwise we couldn't do the jobs that we're hired to do. We're trained, right from umpire school, how to be aggressive, how to take control of a situation, and how to handle problems. Even more important is how to regain your composure, from a mental standpoint, after a big argument or brouhaha, to be able to do a consistent big league job after a blowout. Those are things folks just don't understand about our game. We're just not mechanical on the field. Like players, we have earned our position in the Major Leagues.

Unlike players, umpires don't have statistics. A player can be judged by his .330 batting average but an umpire is evaluated only for his judgment and demeanor on the field. The way umpires handle themselves every day on the field has to do with pride and professionalism. Umpires work hard every day. They have great respect for the greatest game ever invented.

To umpires, ejections are just a part of the game. They have no more significance than balls, strikes, safes, outs, fairs, and fouls. The umpires are charged with seeing that the game runs smoothly to its conclusion. When something out of the ordinary occurs and action needs to be taken, the umpire will do whatever is necessary.

Sometimes, because of a player's actions or disrespect for authority, he will be eliminated from that day's game. I never could understand why a player would become so irate with an umpire's call. I fully understand the competitive spirit but don't understand the loss of composure. Why would a player hurt his own team by acting like an ass and being ejected?

Fans ask all the time, "What is the magic word a player, coach, or manager says to be ejected?" The answer is not what the fans might think. Most think that anytime a player uses a vulgarity he's in danger of ejection. That might be true but it is not automatic. What is automatic during the course of an argument is when a player, coach, or manager prefaces anything with the word "you." The umpire's awareness heightens because anything that follows "you" in an argument is going to be personal. Without doubt an ejection will follow every time.

Bobby Cox was ejected more often than any manager in baseball history. Sure, he managed a long time. But he was thrown out for fighting hard for his team and maybe being a little more boisterous than other people. He was a little more demonstrative in his reactions to things that happened on the field. Bobby was no different than any other manager in that regard; he just went over the top sometimes. Cox won wherever he managed and won wherever he coached. He won fourteen straight divisional titles—a record in any professional sport. If those are not Hall of Fame credentials, then I don't know what are. Bobby may have used salty language but I don't think most umpires cared. That's part of our culture. Four-letter words and combinations of are part of the culture. It's not necessarily church out there on the field. It's competition.

We all are of a competitive mind. We wear athletic supporters. And with that comes salty language. If a player says something to the effect of, "That's a horseshit call. How could you make a stupid fucking call like that?" that's no big deal. That's not an issue whatsoever—at least it wasn't for me and most of the umpires I worked with. What *is* a big deal is when it becomes personal. So if a guy wants to swear, that's fine. If a guy wants to swear about a situation, that's fine. I have no issue with that. But if he gets personal, and swears at me, he will be ejected.

The thing about ejections is this: I'm gonna be there for nine innings. The player doesn't need to be. Where is he more valuable? A player, coach, or manager has an obligation, too, and that is to be as good as he can be, to make his club as good as it can be. Being ejected from that day's game is not giving his team the best opportunity to win. It is his obligation to act with decorum and in a professional manner. The same goes for the umpire. It's a two-way street. And that's why umpires try like hell to maintain their composure in any and all situations. Sometimes it doesn't work. But most times it certainly does.

I don't remember everybody I ejected. I have no clue. I could probably tell you ten or twelve of them, but I know I couldn't tell you half of them.

An umpire once said that if you're going to umpire in the big leagues, you're going to toss over three a year. Circumstance is gonna create it. You're in a decision-making occupation and you're going to piss off some people; they aren't going to like all the decisions you make all the time. They're going to get angry and pissed off and they're going to say some things that perhaps they shouldn't.

I didn't have a "favorite" ejection target. There were guys I didn't get along with or see eye to eye with on everything (like some of my former wives, perhaps). But I wasn't looking to eject them unless they stepped out of line. Play today's game today.

I don't know if alcohol played any part in the outbursts of players or managers I ejected. I know some of them had tobacco breath and some of them had bloodshot eyes. I know I never drank with any managers the night before. I can't in clear conscience condemn a guy for imbibing alcohol when I did the same thing. But when you earn a chance to put on a big league uniform, there's a responsibility that goes along with that. And that responsibility is to do the best you can every single day you put that uniform on. If you're impaired in any way, then you're not doing the best you can.

It's a big deal to look in the mirror and be satisfied with the job you do. If you're not as good as you can be, you're cheating yourself, you're cheating the game, and you're cheating your employers. That's not the way I lived my life in the big leagues. I didn't do it.

MISSED CALLS

Even a sober umpire can make mistakes once in a while.

During my second year, we were in the old open-air ballpark in Bloomington, where the Minnesota Twins were playing the Boston Red Sox. We called Metropolitan Stadium "the Erector Set" because it looked like a kid's erector set on the outside. My position on the field that night was first base. Jerry Remy, the California batter, grounded a ball towards Twins shortstop Roy Smalley. It had been raining off and on and the field was a little slippery. As Smalley fielded the ball and threw to first, I tried to set myself in a good position with an angle. I saw Smalley throw but, as I shifted my weight, my back foot slipped and my head dipped. By the time I recovered, Craig Kusick was holding the ball in his glove and Remy had crossed first base. I had no idea if the runner was safe or out.

This was one of those occasions where an umpire just has to guess. I did but apparently guessed wrong. I called Remy out but was evidently the only person there who didn't see the play. Remy couldn't believe the call. Angels manager Gene Mauch couldn't believe the call. And, by the reaction of the whole ballpark, I figured I'd missed the play. Remy immediately threw his helmet in disgust and earned himself an ejection. Mauch came out to argue but held his composure and was not ejected.

American League president Lee MacPhail, who was in attendance that day, came to visit after the game. He came to my dressing stall and said, "Young fella, that was quite a call at first base." I said, "Yes, sir." He asked, "If you had to make that call again, would you make it in the same way?" With as much false bravado as I could muster, I said, "Yes, sir." MacPhail looked me right in the eye and said, "Young fella, if you called that play the same way, you would have missed it twice."

There are pitches that I missed or that I called incorrectly, but there was never one that I didn't see—unless a catcher stood straight up and blocked my vision. Then I just had to pick one. I either got it right or got it wrong but really couldn't know. Even when I knew I missed a call, I never had a giveback to that player or club. Never. Never. I don't know a Major League umpire who would ever even consider doing that. You miss a play, you miss a call, and you miss it from your heart and not your head. As long as a missed call is not premeditated, there's no issue there. You made a mistake, that's all, and you go on.

Umpires don't have to be told when they make a bad call. Innately, they know it. It's not because of poor judgment. It's because of poor timing. You learn very early in your career that an umpire's best friend is good timing. His worst enemy is anticipation. A play does not have to be called in a split second. You can see the play live. You can see it again in your mind's eye. And then you can call it. You can do the same thing with pitches. See the pitch, see it again, and then call it. That's what makes an umpire a good umpire: not making a call quickly, but calling the play correctly.

When an umpire goes into a dressing room after a game, and he asks his partners if they saw the play the same way, he hopes they tell the truth, not what he wants to hear. He either got it right or got it wrong.

Let's say there's a sliding tag play at second base, and I call the runner out. And then, because the runner rolled over or something, the ball popped out of the fielder's glove and he grabbed it real fast, but I didn't see it. Obviously, the runner should be called safe. But I didn't see it. If I see, out of the corner of my eye, one of the umpires kind of strolling to me, in our crew that was indication that, hey, something happened that I didn't see. Something was going on that I wasn't aware of. "What happened that I didn't see?" "The ball came out of his glove." "Fine. Are you sure?" "Absolutely." I turn around, point at the guy, say "You're safe," indicate that the ball was out of the glove, get ready for an argument, and go on.

THE GOOD UMP

There are ways an umpire can be prepared for every play before it happens. He can look at the defensive players and their positioning. Maybe the outfielders are shading a certain hitter more to right field than straight away. Maybe the shortstop is playing a certain hitter more toward third base. All those little things suggest where a hitter might be inclined to hit the ball because the pitcher is going to work him a certain way. Umpires have to notice those subtle movements and plan positioning that may make the difference between seeing a play clearly or not.

Every team has advance scouts who chart each movement of opposing teams and players they are going to face soon. The scouting reports are relayed to the manager, who determines his strategy on pitching and defense against that opponent. It's the same strategy that umpires talk about while preparing for games in their dressing room. It's hard work—but, like all professionals, they tend to make the job look easy.

Like players, umpires use signals to communicate during games. Partners signal each other to watch for a potential infield fly rule, a timed play, or how the crew will rotate around the bases on a particular hit.

Fans are aware that there is always an umpire at a base but don't realize that it is not always the same one. Sometimes the first base umpire calls a play at second base. Sometimes the third base umpire calls a play at second. Sometimes the home plate umpire calls a play at either first or third. All of that is determined before games by each individual umpiring crew. At Fenway Park, for example, a crew might alter its rotation because of the proximity of the Green Monster in left field.

Umpires are never "the show" but are certainly an integral part of the game. They make the game run smoothly by handling themselves in a cool, calm manner. They recognize potential problems before they fester and will defuse the situation before anyone realizes what might have happened. In virtually every argument, it is not the umpire who is out of control. He's trying to calm the situation and keep the player or manager in the game. It's the umpire who walks away from a confrontation that is explosive. He understands body language and uses psychology on the field as a means of control.

Most fans believe the most difficult place to umpire is behind home plate. Although the home plate umpire does make the most decisions, I believe it is tougher to work second base. The second base umpire has to be aware of multiple situations. He has baseballs hit and thrown in his direction. He has players sliding into second base from first and runners trying to return to second safely on pick-off plays. He sometimes has to go to first base or third base to make calls. And he has to make rulings on shoestring catches in the outfield. Although the home plate umpire has to call hundreds of pitches, he is not moving. He is also wearing a lot of protection, unlike the umpires on the bases.

I think we started to earn respect on the field when advances were made in technology—when instant replay, stop-action, and slow motion were introduced to our game. Those innovations did not show how wrong the umpires were; it actually showed how *right* they were in a huge percentage of their decisions.

If today's advanced technology can be used to help umpires make correct decisions on the field, I'm all for it. Fair or foul balls that hook around a pole are very difficult to see. Video replay can also help determine fan interference and trapped balls in the outfield. Umpires are extraordinarily good at seeing a ball that hits the ground before it is trapped by an outfielder. If it's done appropriately, using technology wouldn't slow down the game any more than an argument does.

I think there's a place for instant replay to go in and see what really happened. That said, I don't think we should use it to call balls and strikes. I don't think we should use it for outs and safes, unless it's a sliding tag play and someone says, "Hey, he dropped the ball." And then only if the umpire didn't see it.

The epitome of virtual replay was the introduction of the Umpire Information System in 2001. Called "QuesTec" after the company that created it, the system consists of four cameras placed strategically around the ballpark. Two are located in the stands along the baselines with the other two at field level. Together, they were supposed to produce digital computer images that could be turned into CDs for umpires and baseball executives to review. In short, they were monitors to check the accuracy of ball-and-strike calls by the home plate umpires.

Used in only six ballparks the first year, QuesTec was controversial from the start because it challenged the integrity of the umpires, or at least their eyes. The system analyzed more than 4,800 games by the end of the 2008 season. Since I retired in

2001, my personal experience with QuesTec was limited. But I know I hated the whole idea.

That's not to say I didn't like some aspects of instant replay. Although QuesTec is bullshit, stop-action and slow motion have value. People can see that umpires are making the correct calls on a consistent basis. Therefore respect is earned not only for the individual umpire but for umpires collectively.

When the pitcher throws the ball, umpires react to what happens on the field. There's absolutely no premeditation by an umpire in how a play, pitch, or anything else on the field is called. It happens, we see it, and we call it. It makes no difference who's in the batter's box—whether it's a left-handed batter or right-handed batter, who the pitcher is, or whether the play is at first base, second base, or third base.

I was not happy when Major League Baseball introduced QuesTec to monitor the strike zone. I thought it was ridiculous, absolutely absurd. First of all, it's impossible to tell on a two-dimensional screen what happens on a three-dimensional field. There's no depth involved. The things that they show on television are just as bad; they give the fans a false impression of what actually is there.

Seldom is the camera used directly in center field. It's off to the left or off to the right, which throws the whole thing out of whack. The more distance you have, even with a magnifying lens, the worse perception you've got. With a two-dimensional camera, you can put that dot anywhere but you don't know whether if it's five feet in front of home plate or three feet behind home plate.

Because the game is being umpired by human beings of different sizes, the perception of where a pitch is will be slightly different. That's why good pitchers and good teams kept books on umpires. They scout umpires the same way they scout players. They would know what Al Clark called in the first inning, as opposed to the ninth inning. How'd he call pitches? As much as we want to be as consistent as we can, sometimes we're not. They wanted to know that. Teams have an edge by knowing that. If the pitcher is good enough, and the scouting report on an umpire is right on, the pitchers will pitch to the umpire. If they know an umpire calls a low strike on the outside, the good pitcher might throw that pitch at just the right time. He gets that one strikeout and the whole picture and complexion of the game changes. Is that wrong? Hell, no, it's not wrong. You just have to remember that the game is being played and officiated by human beings.

INJURIES

Like any umpire, I suffered injuries in the line of duty. The older I got, the more they hurt—and the longer it took to stop hurting.

When you're young, there's a pride thing. You get hit but all you want to do is spit on it, rub it, and continue. It could be a compound fracture in your arm but your attitude is, "Nah, I don't need a trainer. Let's go." But as you get older, it hurts more. I would rather have six arguments than go back there and get hit one time. Those baseballs travel fast, they're hard, and they hurt.

One time in Kansas City, when I was on the foul side of first base, the second baseman fielded a slow roller. The ball sailed away from its intended path and ricocheted off the first baseman's glove, striking me squarely on the forehead. I collapsed on the field and was unconscious for a short time. After coming to, I continued as the first base umpire.

At Baltimore's Memorial Stadium, I was carried off the field on a stretcher one night. Dave Winfield, a big, strong slugger who then played for the Yankees, sliced a line drive down the first base line from the right-handed batter's box. A runner was being held on by the Orioles' first baseman, so I was standing in foul territory, two steps behind the bag. Winfield hit the ball so hard I literally did not have time to respond. The ball struck me on the right inside thigh. I never lost consciousness, but the hit knocked me out of the game and into a local hospital. X-rays showed no broken bones, but I was diagnosed with a deep bruise. It kept me on crutches for a week and off the field for two. The large purple welt on my leg lasted a month and a half.

When I got hit in Milwaukee County Stadium, I was the home plate umpire. When the home plate umpire is injured, the second base umpire will normally replace him and finish the game from that position. That day's second base umpire was Rick Reed. I was wearing an old pair of shin guards that had been taped across the knee area. It may have been superstitious but I didn't want to change equipment in the middle of the season. The injury I suffered in Milwaukee proved I was wrong. When I was hit in the knee, the blow knocked my legs out from underneath me and I flipped forward, landing on my back. Brewers head trainer John Adams came onto the field to tend to my injury while the other umps gathered around home plate to check on their partner. Before he even gave me a chance to get up, Adams said, "Let's go. Let's get him out of here. Rick, you'd better go get your stuff on." And Rick said, "Wait a minute. See if he can get up first." My injuries that day could have been worse; at least home plate umpires wear all kinds of protection, from chest protectors to masks and shin guards. Umpires on the bases have no protection other than their own quick reflexes.

One of my other injuries was my own fault. We were in the old Tiger Stadium in Detroit, and Gregg Jefferies of the Tigers had complained about a third strike. Gregg wasn't the most likable guy. The way he argued and the way he disagreed really was degrading, so I ejected him immediately. But I ejected him with such fervor that I literally snapped one of my hamstrings. Larry Parrish, the Tigers' manager at the time, came out and said, "Jesus, Al, what the hell is going on?" I said, "Larry, I'm not putting up with his shit and you better not get on my ass because I just snapped a hamstring and I'm hurting like hell." He said, "Oh, my God, should I get the trainer?" I said, "No, I'm not going to let anybody know I was hurt." I went back and finished the game behind the plate, a doctor came in afterward and examined me and iced me down, but I worked third base the next day. By the time I got back to working home plate, almost a week later, I had stretched it out and it started to heal. That was the only time I injured myself during an ejection!

Not all mishaps were accidents. Sometimes I was targeted aggressively by fans. I was the home plate umpire in a game at Baltimore which the Orioles lost, through no fault of mine. From the field to the dressing room at Camden Yards, we had to walk on a runway where we were exposed to the fans above. A young woman of nineteen or twenty came rushing toward me. She took a thirty-two-ounce container of beer and poured it on me. That *really* pissed me off.

I got a security guard, found the woman, and made sure she was detained. Every ballpark has a quasi-jail or detention area, and that's where security took her. I was asked to come up and identify her and was asked if I would press charges. I said yes. That terrified her and I was going to let her go. After all, she was just a kid. But while she was still in the cell, she looked at me and gave me the finger. So I said, "Fuck her," and proceeded to press charges against her. Then we went up to Boston and I forgot about it.

It turned out that her family had something to do with Boog Powell, the former Oriole slugger who had a barbecue pit at Camden Yards. Somehow he got through to our dressing room phone in Fenway Park. I didn't have a clue what he wanted. He said, "You know that situation you had in Baltimore with the young lady who threw beer on you? I know her family well and have known them a long time and I think you should just let it go." I said, "Why would I do that?" He said, "I'll send you guys a couple of sandwiches the next time you're in Baltimore." I said, "No, I'm not going to accept a bribe or take a phone call from you in a situation like this." It wasn't a very cordial ending but he hung up.

A month or so later, when I was back in Baltimore, I was called as a witness. The judge reprimanded her and made her do some kind of community service. This young lady was quite frightened.

She had to admit what she did and the judge made her apologize to me in open court.

PRESSURE

Umpires get ready to umpire a Major League game the same way every day. They have the same approach to Seattle vs. Kansas City that they do for New York vs. Boston. We know we've got a job to do, and all games are the same. Home plate doesn't move. If the ball goes over home plate, the pitch is a strike. Umpires, at least 99.5 percent of the time, never get caught up in the media hype. They have a job to do and they do it.

An umpire's mindset every day is this: "This is a great opportunity to shine. Let's go out and do the job we're capable of doing." It's never "Oh, gosh, this is a big game. We've got to be careful of this. We've got to be careful of that."

Umpires also need to protect their integrity. Tom Haller was a catcher for the Tigers while his brother Bill was an American League umpire. There were several occasions when Bill was calling balls and strikes over his brother's shoulder. The only person who ever questioned the Hallers was Earl Weaver, the feisty Baltimore manager. He wanted to know how it could happen that the two of them would be behind the plate together. If he knew either Bill or Tom, he would have known their integrity level surpassed anyone else's on the field—including Weaver's. I'm sure the Hallers had some disagreements but Bill would bend over backward to avoid being accused of nepotism.

No matter which umpires are involved, the media focus in the postseason is so much different than it is during the regular season. There are six guys out there with a little monkey jumping from shoulder to shoulder when plays are occurring. As plays develop, you hope that monkey doesn't land on your shoulder and stay there.

The pressure to be correct and perform right every day is excruciating. The idea that umpires are flawless is a flawed idea.

No one wants to make a mistake. If somebody makes a question-able call during a postseason game, it is just magnified so much. The talking heads, the announcers, are not fair to umpires at all. Or very seldom. That's unfortunate because umpires work just as hard on the field as any manager and coach. Sometimes we make a mistake in judgment or an error of omission. That doesn't mean we should be denigrated by the talking heads. It's all part of the game. That's what makes our game as good as it is, the best game out there. Nobody works harder than umpires. No one has to tell us when we make a mistake. When an umpire makes a mistake, it is absolutely from the heart, not from the head. I just don't think a guy should be chastised or criticized on a personal basis because of that.

For the entirety of his career, Richie Garcia was not just a good umpire but a great umpire. I'm sure if Richie Garcia had a redo of that 1996 Orioles-Yankees playoff game when twelve-year-old Jeffrey Maier's interference resulted in a Derek Jeter home run, he would have tried to get a better view. Instead of running out to right field, he would have stopped; and instead of his head bobbing up and down, he would have had a steadier view. Maybe he would have seen the play differently. I've never spoken to Richie about it so it's all conjecture on my part.

In the 2003 National League Championship Series between the Cubs and Marlins, Steve Bartman didn't do anything any other fan wouldn't have done. He reached for a fly ball in foul territory. When you see a baseball coming at you, you don't think, "I'd better not do this because it might blow the game for my team." In baseball, we call the balls pearls. And pearls are valu-able. That's why you take your glove to the ballpark.

The rules state that if the ball is in the stands and past the line of demarcation, the ball is fair game for fans to catch. If, on the other hand, the fan reaches out over the playing field and costs a player a chance to catch the ball, the umpire can call fan inter-ference. He can rule the batter out or place runners on the bases where they might have advanced without the interference. The fan cannot go onto the playing field but the player can reach into the fan area. In the Bartman game, the Cubs contended Moises Alou could have caught the ball. The umpire didn't see it that way and ruled it a foul ball. Then the roof fell in and the Marlins had a big inning.

In the 2012 ALCS between the Tigers and Yankees, when Omar Infante was called safe sliding back into second base, the umpire (Jeff Kellogg) got blocked a little bit. His eyes may have been at the bag, watching the runner's hand, when in fact the tag occurred on the player's chest. The replay showed the tag was made before the hand got to the bag. Unfortunately it was a blown play.

Jim Joyce is one of the finer, most respected umpires in MLB today. I worked with Jim and know him well. But he admitted he blew the call at first base that deprived Armando Galarraga of a perfect game a few years ago.

Sam Holbrook, on the other hand, was 100 percent correct in calling the infield fly rule during the 2012 Braves-Cardinals wild-card game. The talking heads, even the former players, don't understand the rule or the purpose behind the rule. The rule is to protect the offensive team. When the St. Louis shortstop was back-pedaling and side-pedaling to the outfield, he turned around and had his chest facing the infield. He was calling for the ball, creating a play interpreted as easily handled by an infielder. At that point, and only at that point, should the infield fly rule be called. That's what Holbrook did. He waited until the ball was on the way down from its apex, and until the infielder had turned around, and then called it an infield fly. That the shortstop and left fielder miscommunicated has no bearing on the umpire's call.

Had the left fielder made the play, fired it to third, and the third baseman thrown it to second, there would have been a double play. At that juncture, the Braves would have argued that the infield fly rule *should* have been called. But that call is not the reason the Braves lost the game. Very rarely does one call by an umpire make the difference in a game.

Since we are constantly at risk for injuries in addition to abusive behavior by players and fans, umpires need a good sense of humor.

In our dressing room, nothing was off limits, including weight. I worked with three other guys who were rather large: Larry Barnett, Greg Kosc, and Dan Morrison. We had a running thing in the dressing room: the first guy who bent down to tie his shoes would be "courteous" and ask the other guys if they needed anything while we were down here. And I had three wives, so that made me a pretty good target, too. We could rag on each other. But if an outsider walked into that dressing room, he'd better not try it. The umpires are family; I not only worked with those guys but ate with them, traveled with them, laughed with them, and cried with them.

We laughed a lot.

One spring training my friends Alfie Rossi and Woody Woolwine were seated along the third base side. The game started at 1:00 but we had a 4:30 tee time. I was working home plate but tried to keep an eye on Alfie and Woody. With the score tied late in the game, Alfie looked at me and pointed at his watch, which read 3:45. Lo and behold, the first guy up in the bottom of the ninth got a hit, the second guy walked, the third guy popped up, and the fourth guy hit a bleeder to right field. The guy on second never broke stride coming home, where there was a play at the plate. The throw was a little bit to the first base side and caused a huge cloud of dust as the catcher scrambled to make the tag. When the dust cleared, the runner was safe, and we made our tee time.

There was another time when we had to leave early for golf. It was the seventh or eighth inning and the score wasn't even close. The other team tied it up going into the ninth. We were going to be late. I walked over to the visitors' dugout, asked the manager if he had more pitchers, and learned he did not. So I declared, "Game over, out of pitchers."

I was in Fort Lauderdale in 1997 to umpire a spring training game between the Yankees, who then trained there, and the Atlanta Braves, who were up the interstate in West Palm Beach. Andruw Jones had just had a great first season with the Braves, becoming the youngest player to homer in a World Series. Before the game, I was relaxing outside our dressing room, which happened to be adjacent to the visitors' clubhouse in Fort Lauderdale Stadium. Andruw was out there in uniform, standing in an area accessible to fans, but was blowing off all the kids begging for his autograph. I didn't think that was quite right.

I said, "Andruw, why don't you sign some of those youngsters' autographs for them?" He turned around, not knowing who I was. I was in street clothes, not in umpire gear, and was obviously older than he. He looked at me quizzically, not knowing what to think, but reluctantly signed some autographs.

I went about my business until the game began. Andruw came up in the first inning and I knew he still hadn't recognized me. I called time, turned around to brush off home plate, stood straight up, and took off my mask. I turned to Andruw so he could see my face and said to him, "*Now* aren't you glad you signed those autographs?" For a second, there was a quizzical look on his face. Then he realized I was the home plate umpire and the person who told him to sign before. All of a sudden that big, wide, gracious smile came across Andruw's face. Hopefully he was a little mellower when it came time to signing youngsters' autographs from that time forward.

Although I got the attention of Andruw Jones, I'm not sure about Mickey Rivers.

From the dugout to the field in the old Yankee Stadium, the field pitched because it needed to drain when it rained. That ballpark didn't have the great drainage system that the new fields have. The rain would flow from both sides of the pitcher's mound and then wash into the dugout and down the drains. As a result, it was impossible to see third base from the first base dugout. You could stand on the top step and *almost* see third base. But if you were in the dugout, there was no way.

Mickey Rivers was on second base one day when a ball was hit to right-center field. Rivers, a very fast guy, took off. He rounded third, where I was working, and I saw that he missed the base. He raced across the plate and nothing was said. Then George Brett, star third baseman of the visiting Kansas City Royals, made his move. He called time and put the ball back into play the correct way. The pitcher went to the rubber, stepped off, threw to third base, and appealed to me that Rivers had missed third base.

Since I saw it, I called him out, nullifying the run. Billy Martin came running out to third base and said, "What the hell is going on?" I said, "Billy, he missed third base." He said, "Jesus, how could he miss third?" I said, "I don't know, but he did." Billy didn't argue that much but did say, "I'm gonna get back there, and I'm gonna fine his ass." Evidently he did.

That winter I went to a dinner where Mickey Rivers was speaking. Before it started we were at a cocktail party. Mickey came up to me and said, "Hey, Al. You cost me a hundred bucks." I said, "What do you mean?" He said, "Remember that day you called me out for missing third base?" I said, "Yeah." He said, "Billy fined me a hundred bucks for that and I'm never going to forget it."

PRIDE

When interleague play began in 1997, we saw different teams. It didn't make any difference because we saw all the teams in spring training anyway. The big change came two years later when the umpiring staffs were mixed as well. All of a sudden, we went to all the cities and all the ballparks in MLB. I think the old school guys were more opposed to it than the younger umpires.

I was proud to be an American League umpire. But I was also proud to be a *Major League* umpire. It was the same for the National League guys who were proud to be National League umpires.

For twenty-four years, except for showcase assignments in Philadelphia and San Francisco, I had made friends only in American League cities. I knew the restaurants and the restaurant employees. I knew the hotel people. There was a comfort level in traveling to cities we frequented five or six times during the season. Fortunately, the umpire supervisors were wise enough to integrate the previously separated league umpires. That made going to new cities easier. At first, half the umpires didn't even know the route to the dressing rooms at the different ballparks. We relied on each other. Today's young umpires never experienced the separation of the league umpiring staffs and don't know the ways of the past.

TRAVEL

Traveling gets more difficult as you get older. If a person had to start traveling in his late forties, for example, I don't know if he'd be physically or mentally capable of doing it. I think a person who travels has to learn how to travel *as a business*. And I think he's got to learn that in his formative years. Otherwise, it becomes very difficult.

Experience is a great teacher, especially when it comes to giving tips to travelers. Who better to learn about traveling from than a road warrior who's been on the road for seven months a year for thirty years?

When staying in a hotel, it is much better to sleep in a hotel bed on the opposite side of where the telephone is. The simple reason is that most everyone who checks into a hotel sleeps next to the phone. The mattress is firmer on the opposite side of the bed.

Here's another tip: when you get into your hotel room and request a wake-up call, put the phone on the floor. That way, you've got to actually swing your arms and legs out of bed, bend down, and pick up the phone. Once your feet are on the floor, you're more likely to actually get up instead of going back to sleep.

One of the first things I do when I check into a hotel room is check the nightstand and take out the Bible. Many times, people hide their cash in Bibles—and then forget to take it with them. I have found thousands of dollars over the years.

We always made our own travel arrangements. Baseball provided only a schedule with cities and dates on it—our assignments. It was our job to do airplanes, cars, or hotels. We were our own travel agencies. That was a very positive thing for umpires. We got to know a lot of people on a personal basis in the travel and hospitality industry.

We were sent first-class, point-to-point, open airplane tickets. And all we had to do was make our own reservations. And until Pilot Air Freight started moving our equipment in the '80s, we had to take our equipment with us. Even after that, until MLB worked out some customs issues, we had to carry our equipment into and out of Toronto and Montreal. It was a terrible pain in the neck. Now the guys never touch their equipment bags.

Our travel objective was to be in the next city an hour and a half before the ballgame. It didn't make any difference how we got there. Sometimes we flew together, sometimes we didn't. Sometimes we ate together, sometimes we didn't. The people on crews are work partners. They're not life partners. When people go to the office, they don't go home with their work partners that night.

Whenever I negotiated a hotel rate, one of my main points was that we umpires were the best guests the hotels would ever have. We're frequent travelers, we don't wreck rooms, we're repeat customers, we pay our bills, and we eat and drink in the hotel. If you're a hotel executive, isn't that your perfect guest?

Players have everything done for them; most have no idea how to travel on their own. Remember Willie Mays Aikens? When the players went on strike in 1981, Willie asked Dean Vogelaar, traveling secretary of the Royals, what time the team bus was leaving the stadium for the airport. But the player strike canceled everything—not only games but bus rides.

Our equipment was sometimes a no-show, too. In fact, it happened about three or four times a year. When that happened the home club supplied us with groundskeepers' uniforms—they were kind of neutral—and catcher's protective equipment—masks, shoes, and spikes. Whatever it took to suit up for a game. We did look kind of funny, wearing the home team hats. But they tried to distinguish us by giving us the "away" hat. It had a logo on it but was usually a different color. We hated it when it happened. But two or three times when you're making sixty or seventy or seventy-five trips in the summertime is not really that bad.

The only good reason for a crew to be late for a game is that the transportation system has broken down—if there's bad weather and the airplanes aren't flying. It's usually because of thunderstorms in the summertime or flying into or out of Minneapolis, Toronto, or Denver in the springtime. One of the worst situations was when we were flying from Newark to Chicago in the summer. We taxied out and thunderstorms—or the threat of thunderstorms—came. We went to what they call a bullpen area to wait for an active runway—and for the storms to subside. We sat there three and a half hours. They wouldn't let us take off given the threat of thunderstorms not only there but also in our destination city. I understand the importance of safety—but, wow, that was a hard experience. That was one of the toughest things about traveling.

Getting through security was another hassle. Once the Kansas City club was leaving to go on a trip and a bus took the team right out onto the tarmac, where they got on the plane. I asked a friend who worked for United Airlines how the players got through security. He said, "Oh, they have some TSA people that go right to the ballpark, check their bags, and check the bus. They do it at the ballpark so they can go straight onto the tarmac."

That was a convenience we never experienced. I've talked to guys since 9/11 who say that depending upon what city they're in and depending upon what time of day they're traveling, the security is absolutely hit and miss. Sometimes you can get through in ten or fifteen minutes and other times it can take up to two hours. Therein lies one of the hardships of traveling in today's world. I understand that it's necessary, but it's a real pain. I really think profiling should be employed—the way they do it in Israel. You know, if it looks like a rose and smells like a rose, maybe it is a rose.

Renting a car is a lot easier than flying. Umpires get two car rentals per crew. We used to get none and then just one once in a while. Hey, times change. That's progress.

INNOVATORS

I am a big fan of new ideas that might help the game.

I worked a ballgame in Oakland with orange balls and orange bases. It didn't work because you couldn't see them at night. It was a great idea and, pardon the pun, added color to the game. But the bases got dirty and the fans couldn't see them. That was just one of the ideas introduced by Charlie Finley, owner of the Oakland A's in the '70s. He was also the guy who introduced colorful nicknames and multicolored uniforms and mascots. He also helped umpires by providing a mechanical rabbit that would supply us with new baseballs during games. It was hidden in the ground but appeared like a jack-in-the-box when we needed it.

Bill Veeck was another maverick. He tried all kinds of things with the various teams he owned, from the Cleveland Indians to the St. Louis Browns and Chicago White Sox. Veeck was in Chicago when he dressed his team in short pants and shirts with collars. Maybe it made them look like a softball team, but it played pretty well. And like Finley, Bill Veeck helped umpires. He created a nozzle that emitted pressurized air to clean off home plate. It just didn't work as well as my trusty brush.

George Steinbrenner was involved with umpires, too. He probably sent more tapes criticizing or ostracizing umpires to the American League office than any owner. But, then again, there weren't many owners like George Steinbrenner. Take the bluster away from the Boss and he was a pretty good guy. And who could blame a guy who owned the New York Yankees, or any team, if he just wanted to win?

That was the public side of George. Privately he was one of the most giving and charitable people that you could possibly imagine. An umpire who happened to live near Steinbrenner's home in Florida had a family tragedy. George found out about it and sent his private plane so the umpire could take his child to the Mayo Clinic in Rochester, Minnesota. No one hears about that. He was a very generous guy.

ADVICE

I have not gone to games since I left baseball. However I do watch games on television, talk with some other umpires once in awhile, and run into active and retired players at dinners during the off-season. I read the newspapers every day and the Internet all the time, just to keep up.

I always look for the names of the umpires in the box scores. I never stopped. I've seen the coming of the new guard, names I don't recognize. That's the sort of transition that happens not only on the baseball field but in life. The new guard is here and hopefully they are good—and better than we were. They've got more on the ball, they pay attention better, they learn things from us. If they're better umpires, the game is going to be officiated more efficiently. And that will make it a better game. I just want our game to be as good and as strong as it can possibly be.

The truth is it's not easy being a professional umpire. In any sport being a big league official takes a lot of work, dedication, and sacrifice. You've got to love the game and love officiating. You've got to love every minute of it. There is no mental down time. A Major League official thinks about the job 24/7. There is no real off-season because wherever you go, there are fans everywhere who want to talk about your job.

People always want to know what advice I would give to anyone who wants to be an umpire. The first thing I would do would ask that person if he or she is willing to make a lot of sacrifices in life. It is hard to be away from home through the Minor Leagues, and through the big leagues, in a career that could span thirty to forty years. The sacrifices are plentiful. You miss time with families; you miss Little League games, football games, and school plays and concerts. You're away for seven months a year. That's very difficult, and not very many people are willing to create that kind of life for themselves.

Then I would ask them why. If the person says, "Because I'm a baseball fan and I want to be close to the players," that is probably the *worst* reason to become an umpire. But if a guy says he's a Type A personality who likes to be in control, that's another thing. He has to love to handle situations and to be on top of things. Then I would suggest he go to umpire school, develop and hone those skills, and see where his attitude and ability take him.

4 Dressing the Part

Players are choosy and care about their equipment, and umpires are the same way. Umpires procure all their own equipment: chest protector, shin guards, steel-toed shoes for protection, and masks. The only item MLB supplies is the actual cloth uniforms.

In the Minor Leagues we had to buy everything ourselves, but in the big leagues companies asked us to wear their equipment, which was like free advertising for them. Anything we asked for from a manufacturer was given to us. Gloves for cold weather were also provided. In my day we had nice, heavy gloves with a big American League logo on them. I gave them to my brother Marty, who still uses them in his ball games in and around New Jersey.

There are a couple of umpires in the equipment business. Joe West has his West Vest, a protective chest protector. Gerry Davis has a whole array of equipment for professionals and amateurs. Before that, former National League ump Paul Pryor used to sell umpire equipment. He may have been the only outlet at that time.

I signed a contract with a company called PLUS POS that supplied equipment to umpires all over the world. I was very fortunate; I designed and had an autographed set of my own shin guards, Al Clark–model umpire shin guards. A player might have an autographed glove or a model bat. As an umpire, I had autographed shin guards. They retailed for $116 in the 1980s. I designed them. Earlier-style shin guards had just a piece of stiff leather at the knee joint. Mine had a shield that protected the knee joint. I had a very nice relationship with PLUS POS.

When our equipment started to get a little frayed, we gave it to young, struggling Minor League umpires who could not afford to buy their own. Major League umpires have always done that.

My first umpire's travel case was made by a Cincinnati outfit called Priestmeyer and Company. It was like a big steamer case with a tray in it. On the bottom would go shoes, shin guards, chest protector, and mask; and in the tray would go soft clothes. I took it from city to city. It was perfect for umpire gear but even better for a college kid taking his clothes to school and THEN using the trunk as a coffee table in his room. I've given many of my Priestmeyers to my friends' kids.

The airlines were tough on those trunks; they threw them around. Sometimes we needed two in a year. On mine were stenciled my name and the words "American League Umpire." The first Priestmeyer I had was given to me by great NL umpire John Kibler. He was a great gentleman and I was very proud to use his Priestmeyer.

American League Umpires wore red coats for two years, 1976 and 1977, and then we went to a blue double-knit jacket. Those red coats became collector's items. Those were the only years umpires wore anything other than blue serge or a blue coat. We looked like the guys Paul Revere saw when he warned Boston that the British were coming.

Today's big league umps dress with style. There are MLB logos on their caps and on their shirts—signs of professionalism for sure.

Before American League and National League umpire staffs merged in 1999, I was the only person in professional sports ever to wear his name on his cap. Once the staffs merged, I couldn't wear the AL cap anymore. The hats that they've got now are very good but I enjoyed having my name on my hat. I had no complaints about the merger.

Being a Major League umpire as opposed to an American League umpire allowed me the rare treat of working in three special ballparks on consecutive days. It was thrilling even for a crusty old bastard like me at the end of my career. Our crew was scheduled to travel from Chicago to Baltimore with an off day. We had been assigned a makeup game in Boston on a Thursday. So on consecutive days, I worked in Wrigley Field, Fenway Park, and Camden Yards. That was pretty cool.

Umpires now go to all thirty ballparks. They wear black shirts, blue shirts, or red shirts; gray pants, always coordinated; windbreakers; and can choose either long-sleeved or short-sleeved shirts. No longer will you find an umpire in the big leagues wearing a big, heavy wool coat with a shirt, tie, and heavy wool slacks. Those days are gone, just like the old wool uniforms the players used to wear.

Today's fans can barely recall the days when outside chest protectors were used. The last time I used an old, outside, balloon-style chest protector was my first season in the Venezuelan Winter League. But after that the league decided that American League umpires would no longer wear that piece of equipment. The outside protector would be grandfathered out; guys who were wearing it then could wear it until they retired. Umpires promoted after 1975 would wear the inside protector. That may have been the very first step toward the combining of the separate umpire staffs.

Another piece of equipment I used had no monetary value whatsoever. But it was very valuable to me. I started using a brush, a home plate whisk broom, while working in the Class A Midwest League in 1972. As it kept getting worn down, I put more and more tape on the handle. It kept getting shorter as the years went on. I used it through the Midwest League, Texas League, American Association, Florida Instructional League, Venezuelan Winter League, playoffs, All-Star Games, and eight years in the big leagues before I worked a World Series. The first time I worked the plate in a World Series game, the third game of the 1983 Series between Philadelphia and Baltimore, was the last game for the brush. That little brush traveled with me all those years and now occupies a shadow frame in a place of honor in my home.

To me it represents a lot of hard work, sacrifice, and success; and it's one of my most prized possessions.

Glasses were also an important part of my dress on the field. I was the first umpire in the big leagues to wear glasses on an everyday basis.

I was twenty-seven when I was promoted to the big leagues but forty when my vision became a problem. I was working second base in Kansas City when I turned around to see that huge scoreboard at Kauffman Stadium and discovered the numbers were fuzzy. I thought, "Whoa, this is not cool." I went and got my eyes checked. Sure enough, I needed glasses. I had tried to work with contacts but couldn't do it. Many guys wore contacts—umpires, players, coaches, and managers—but they weren't for me. I was always afraid one or the other, or both, would pop out of my eye(s) and then I'd be in trouble. So I wore glasses.

I knew I would be ridiculed on the field by fans. I was ready for that and knew I could deal with that. But I wasn't ready to take ridicule from players, coaches, and managers.

It didn't take long before my wearing glasses became fodder for disputed calls. Our crew was at Yankee Stadium with the Angels the visiting team. Marcel Lachemann was California's pitching coach. I was working first base when the home plate umpire asked for assistance on a checked swing by one of the Yankees players. I ruled no swing, which drew the ire of Lachemann. He climbed to the top step of the visitors' dugout and pointed to my glasses. He raised both arms and summarily dismissed me as inconsequential.

Umpires don't like that and I was no exception. I called time, took a few steps toward home plate, and ejected Lachemann. My ploy worked perfectly. The ejection and its rationale received plenty of attention on ESPN that evening. Most baseball folks saw it. I was never hassled about wearing glasses again.

Other umpires soon started wearing glasses with no issues. Hell, NFL officials wear glasses. Some NBA guys have worn glasses. It's just a matter of becoming a little bit older and needing some aid, some help with your eyes.

There was another glasses incident. We were in Baltimore when it started to drizzle. Anybody who wears glasses knows that a light mist or drizzle interferes with glasses. It's kind of a pain in the ass to keep them clean. I was working second base, positioned on the infield grass on the first base side of second base. To eliminate the drizzle and have clear vision, I took my glasses off and put them in my pocket. All of a sudden, I heard from behind me, on my left, someone requesting time. I quickly turned and saw little Chuck Knoblauch, the Yankees second baseman, coming toward me. Chuck straddled up next to me and he said, "Al, I hope you don't mind, but would you please put your glasses back on?"

I knew we had gone full circle, from an umpire wearing glasses for the first time to being completely accepted. A player actually said, "We know the situation and we want you as good as you can be. Please put your glasses back on."

Plenty of star players wear glasses. Just think about Reggie Jackson and Dick Allen, players who won MVP awards. There's just a myth that umpires are blind and *need* glasses. When one of them actually put a pair on, it seemed out of character. But everything certainly became clear.

5 My Office

For twenty-six years I was lucky to have my office on a large diamond, surrounded by a vast expanse of green, and enough seating to have a terrific party.

I was very fortunate in my career. I worked on crews that were assigned to the closing day in a great old ballpark, Cleveland Stadium, and opening days in Camden Yards, the Jake in Cleveland, and the Ballpark in Arlington. That was kind of cool.

Later in my career, I was glad to see the design trends in modern ballparks. In the '60s and '70s, we had cookie-cutter ballparks. You could close your eyes, take a couple of 360-degree turns, and you really didn't know if you were in Philadelphia, Pittsburgh, St. Louis, or Cincinnati. The multi-purpose stadiums were boring.

When Camden Yards was built, it had a personality all its own. It reflected the city, the area. If you closed your eyes at the Inner Harbor, made a turn, and opened your eyes in Camden Yards, you saw the warehouse and the big Bromo-Seltzer clock. You knew you were in Baltimore, with all its nooks and crannies.

The same is true of so many of the new ballparks: the Jake in Cleveland, the Ballpark in Arlington, Coors Field in Colorado. What could be more personal and fun than to go to the ballpark in Denver and see the Rocky Mountains in the distance and the big spruce and fern trees growing beyond the center-field wall? What could be better than going to Houston and seeing the steam locomotive on top of the left-field wall and the incline in center? It reminded me of old Crosley Field in Cincinnati and Forbes Field in Pittsburgh. The new fields create opportunities for general managers to build their ball clubs to suit their ballparks. Doesn't that add good stuff for fans to think about and talk about?

The basketball court hasn't changed in size in a long time. Players are so big and strong the game is almost played above the rim. The people sitting on the floor are constantly looking up. The players on the second level are looking at the basket from eye level.

In football the field is the same and you have twenty-two unbelievably huge and behemoth men moving at the same time. How do you follow that game and know what's going on unless you've got a football-educated mind? But even then, you can't watch everything at the same time.

But you can ask for a certain place in the baseball stadium and know you're going to see your favorite right fielder, your favorite third baseman, or your favorite pitcher. You identify with the ballpark.

People with season tickets get the same seats year in and year out because they like the vantage point. The different dimensions add personality to our game. We enjoy greater diversity because of different stadiums. In Boston the left fielders have to learn to play the wall. In Houston they've got the terrace. There are so many different things. You can go to any ballpark and pick out those things that make our game and the experience unique.

Domed stadiums certainly fit that description. The Tropicana Dome, home of the Tampa Bay Rays, covers various catwalks and speakers that hang from the roof. If you hit some catwalk in foul territory, the ball is always foul. If you hit it past a certain point and the ball lands in fair territory, the ball's in play. I saw Frank Thomas hit a speaker in left-center field and lose a long hit because the ball landed in foul territory. It would have been a home run but was deemed to be foul. The speaker was in fair territory in left-center field. What counted was the striking point on the ground.

The home club sets the ground rules for every ballpark; the umpires just abide by the rules that are set. On the back of all the lineup cards, for home team and visitors, is an outline of the ground rules for that ballpark. The umpires don't change them; the home clubs have to change them. That doesn't happen in football because of the field or basketball because of the court. But baseball has plenty of personality and controversy.

Yogi Berra was right: it ain't over 'til it's over. How many times have we seen the visiting club ahead in the bottom of the ninth inning with two outs and two strikes? One more pitch, one more strike, one more out, and the game is over. Didn't it happen a couple of times in the 2011 World Series between Texas and St. Louis? It happened because there is no clock in baseball and the game has to be played to its conclusion.

For those new to baseball, the game may be hard to figure out. We've got a foul line that should be called a fair line because it is fair when the ball hits it. The same goes for the foul pole; it should be the fair pole because when the ball hits it, it is fair. Our game is so good and so unique in so many different ways that it's fun to have been a baseball fan and now a fan of baseball, certainly for the rest of my life.

In the American League Detroit and Boston have the most ardent fans, and probably St. Louis in the National League, but there isn't one city in the country where the fans are not on top of their game. In the cities I mentioned, the fans might be a bit more vocal. Even at Yankee Stadium, after the fans in right field chant the players' names, it's not quite the same as the constant ballpark din of Detroit or Boston. Give the people in Detroit anything to cheer about and there are thirty-five thousand people in the ballpark every day. Boston fans are so spread out across the New England states that they're called Red Sox Nation.

I didn't have the opportunity to work in Philadelphia until late in my career but I grew up watching the Phillies and their fans. It's pretty tough to downplay a reputation for booing Santa Claus.

The oldest ballparks, Wrigley Field and Fenway Park, are great for the fans, giving them the ambience and the closeness that make fans feel part of the scene. But it's a good thing fans don't deal with the actual infrastructure; the facilities are ancient.

As umpires, we were glad to work anywhere. We were in the Major Leagues! But we are human, too, and were exposed to the elements. Those elements are sometimes overwhelming: cold conditions in April and October; heat and humidity in the middle of the summer; and rain, snow, hail, wind, and lots of thunder and lightning at any time throughout the season. Games have been delayed or canceled because of rain, snow, sleet, hail, lightning, fog, hurricanes, tornadoes, and even earthquakes. In Denver, players tire more quickly because of the altitude. There's even a seat in Coors Field painted a special color to denote the exact spot where the Mile High City is a mile high: 5,280 feet. The combination of Midwestern heat and humidity and artificial turf always posed problems in midsummer. In fact, it always seemed that the Texas Rangers wilted in the heat of the Dallas–Fort Worth area. Who could play baseball when the average temperature is 105 degrees?

Something must have changed, though, since the Rangers have since reached the World Series twice. Maybe it was a little bit of Nolan Ryan or maybe a little bit of Ron Washington. They changed the culture and turned the heat around. Instead of being a detriment to their ball club, it became a benefit. They decided to thrive in the heat and let the visiting clubs suffer.

An old umpire adage is that you can't do anything about precipitation until it arrives. Then you can't do anything about it until it stops. You just try to keep the batter's box and pitcher's mound dry, along with the rest of the infield. Groundskeepers will work with the umpires. They'll say, "Hey, listen, it's going to rain hard in ten minutes and it's going to rain for a half hour." The umpires can stop the game, save the field by getting it covered, take the cover off, and have the field look like it never rained. Today's drainage systems are so good that ten minutes after a downpour ends, the teams can be playing on bone-dry fields.

The decision to start a game is made by the home club—except in the last series of the year between the two clubs. Once the line-ups are exchanged, the umpires are in charge. That way, any potential manipulating of the game by the home club cannot be done. Baseball uses whatever means it can to guarantee the integrity of the game.

I remember managers, general managers, and teams becoming very irate when the umpires stopped games when the rain just started, especially if it was right around the fifth inning. In a Yankee-Baltimore series at old Memorial Stadium, Orioles manager Earl Weaver came out with a mop and was literally mopping up water around the first base area. He wanted to play the game because he was losing by one run. He didn't want the game to be called. It was a silly sight but just one of many I saw during my long career.

The one thing I didn't expect to encounter was a volcano—especially an erupting one. But that was before I crossed paths with Mount St. Helens on May 18, 1980. Our crew was flying from Minneapolis to Seattle when the captain told us half the mountain had been blown off. When Mount St. Helens erupted initially, it diverted many flights. We were fortunate to be on one of the last flights to leave Minneapolis for Seattle that day. As the volcano began erupting, we were flying on the opposite side of the mountain, away from the wind, out of the path of the blowing ash. We got a clear view of a mountain that had blown its top.

The plane had to be diverted around the volcano because it was still pluming ash. From five miles up, we saw the volcano continuing to erupt. I realized I was looking down into an active volcano. The thought of seeing that natural phenomenon is burned into my memory. It was one of the most dramatic things that I had ever seen. Once again, Mother Nature proved to be bigger and stronger than any defense man might deploy against her.

When we landed at Sea-Tac, the Seattle-Tacoma International Airport, it was covered in ash. They had to use snowplows and rotating brushes to remove the ash from the runways. The wind had blown the plume Seattle's way and everything was gray.

The volcano was the talk of the town, the Pacific Northwest, and the whole country. Because of its moist climate, that part of the country was usually blanketed by deep green foliage. Mount St. Helens changed all that. We learned later just how deadly the eruption had been. It killed fifty-seven people and thousands of animals, dropped ash into eleven states, and caused more than a billion dollars in property damage. The volcano destroyed several hundred houses plus enough wood to build thousands more.

Mount St. Helens was not only the largest volcanic eruption in the Lower 48 since before World War I, but also the deadliest and most destructive in American history. Because it released thermal energy 1,600 times greater than the atomic bomb dropped on Hiroshima, I wasn't surprised when President Carter called it "a moonscape" when he flew over the stricken area. It was that dramatic.

I was working with Jimmy Evans's crew at that time. We were scheduled to work in Seattle the day after Mount St. Helens erupted the first time. The Kingdome was not the most beautiful ballpark in the world, but we were grateful it had a roof. Most of the ash stayed outside, except for whatever came in on the shoes of the fans and the people who worked in the stadium.

It was a tough couple of days in Seattle. There were pictures in the paper and on television of how volcanic ash had covered everything. Even though Seattle is usually one of the most picturesque and photogenic cities in the Major Leagues, it was all gray after the volcano.

I gathered a souvenir: a little Gerber baby food jar full of volcanic ash from Mount St. Helens. I still have it today.

Although the first eruption was the worst, it was not the last.

We flew south to Anaheim after that series. The volcano had stopped erupting but ignited again as we were leaving to go down the coast. Instead of flying out of Seattle and heading straight south, we flew due west, way out over the Pacific Ocean, then south to get back to the Los Angeles area. We had to get away from the plume of Mount St. Helens again. All we saw was another cloud of volcanic ash coming west toward the city of Seattle. Those were very impressive, memorable times.

I remember reading about what happened and how it happened in the newspapers. I still have the papers in my personal collection. Despite the devastation the volcano caused, to be part of that was pretty damn cool.

It was a lot more than just another day in the life of an umpire.

6 Names and Games

The goal of every professional umpire is to reach the Major Leagues. After that, the next best thing is to be recognized for his work. Being assigned to the World Series in 1983 was the culmination and the pinnacle of everything I worked for.

Players talk about earning a world championship ring. They say they play for the ring and the money doesn't count. Of course the money counts! But they spend the money and the ring is forever. The ring is a source of pride. It is a sign of tremendous success. It is the way of sustaining what each man started. When he earns it, he's reached a goal. It's the same for umpires. You've reached the pinnacle when you've earned a World Series ring as an umpire. Wearing that ring signifies membership in a very exclusive club.

My most memorable World Series assignment is my first one, Baltimore vs. Philadelphia in 1983. There's something about that first one that makes it special. I wear the '83 World Series ring and have several other rings from showcase events in a safe deposit box.

The commissioner's office allows us to buy the top section of the ring, since it can be made into a charm for a spouse or parent. It reads "World Series Umpire" around the crown, surrounding a nice diamond, and on both sides it has the names of the teams that participated in that World Series, along with the year and the umpire's name. I purchased one for my mom and had inscribed it appropriately on the back. After she passed away, I retrieved it. Just to stay close to her, I wear what I had given her on a chain around my neck.

I've earned two All-Star and two World Series rings. I was able to buy a duplicate set for my dad. Great pride came from giving my dad the same rings I'd earned. That he wore them made me more proud. Most of the rings are earmarked for my nephews. That will be part of the legacy I'll leave for them.

For World Series umpiring crews, Major League Baseball tries to select a couple of young umpires, a couple with a few years behind them, and a couple of senior umpires so there's never a year when an All-Star or postseason game lacks experienced officials. With the turnover and rotation of guys going in and guys going out, there are always veteran umpires assigned. It's obviously a good system. It doesn't mean umps won't make mistakes, but the odds are diminished with experience.

Umpires assigned to special events such as the All-Star Game, playoffs, and World Series are very proud to have been selected. Six umpires work all postseason games; two of them are assigned to work the foul lines. The crew chiefs are picked based on seniority.

Only once was I assigned as a crew chief in a special event. It was the 1994 All-Star Game in Arlington. But I didn't work home plate. One of my partners for that game was fellow American League umpire Durwood Merrill. His hometown was Texarkana, Texas, and he had fifty relatives and neighbors joining him in Arlington that night.

After assignments were made and Durwood learned he was not the senior ump, he called AL Supervisor of Umpires Marty Springstead and asked if assignments could be changed so that he could work the plate in front of his people. Springstead reminded Merrill that "Clarkie" was the senior AL ump assigned to the game and would be the home plate umpire. He also told Durwood that he could ask if I minded switching with him.

Springstead passed on Durwood's request. Given the game's proximity to Merrill's home, and since it was July in Texas, I saw no reason not to switch positions and work second base that night.

When the game started about 7:20 central time, the thermometer read a robust 107 degrees. It was still at 105 when the game ended. Durwood was completely dehydrated after the game. It took him a full twenty minutes to get out of his umpire gear. It was hot and humid at second base, too, but not nearly as toasty as it was behind the plate. It was another good call by a senior umpire.

Of all the showcase games to which I was assigned, the one that meant the most to me was Game Three of the 1983 World Series, at Veterans Stadium in Philadelphia. I will remember that for the rest of my life. It was my first home plate assignment in the World Series. It was also the first time that former Cy Young Award winners opposed each other as starting pitchers in a World Series game: Mike Flanagan for Baltimore and Steve Carlton for Philadelphia. Another former Cy Young Award winner, Jim Palmer, turned out to be the winning pitcher after pitching two innings in relief. It was the last game he would win in the big leagues.

I was very emotional about being there. From the moment I placed a mask on my head at umpire school, I had strived to be in that exact situation. It was an "Oh, what a feeling" moment. The feeling might be duplicated later on but it could never be surpassed.

In my eighth year in the big leagues, I had already worked a couple of playoffs, including the Bucky Dent game in '78, and an American League Championship Series. I did not work an All-Star Game until '84, in San Francisco. But working the World Series was the culmination—more so than signing my first big league contract—of all the hard work, the training, the travel, and those years in the Minor Leagues.

The umpires' World Series rotation is usually based on seniority. That's how I was assigned to work the third game of that Series behind the plate. I had never worked in the Vet before or even seen a game there. Our assignment for the 1983 World Series opener was Marty Springstead at home, Ed Vargo at first, me

1. It's spring training 1976, before Al Clark has even umpired his first regular-season game, but he's already arguing with Yankees manager Billy Martin (left). The original caption reads, "Billy! Behave yourself—it's Sunday." (© Corbis)

2. A little guy with a big mouth, Al Clark locked horns with many managers, including Joe Torre. (Al Clark collection)

3. A's pitcher Dennis Eckersley celebrates as Al Clark calls Brett Butler out to end the 1989 "Earthquake" World Series, a four-game Oakland sweep over San Francisco. (© Bettmann/Corbis)

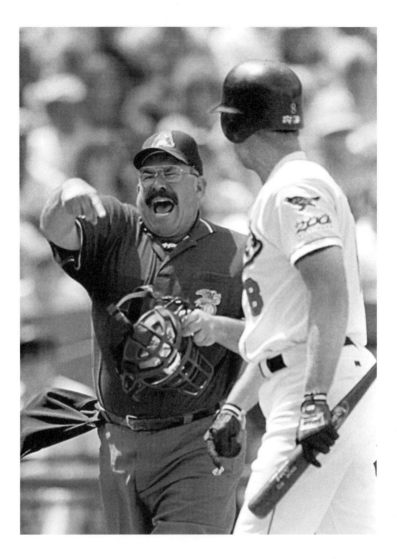

4. Mild-mannered ironman Cal Ripken Jr. loses his cool on July 20, 1997, and loses this argument to Al Clark, the third and last umpire to eject him. (© Ted Mathias/AFP/Getty Images)

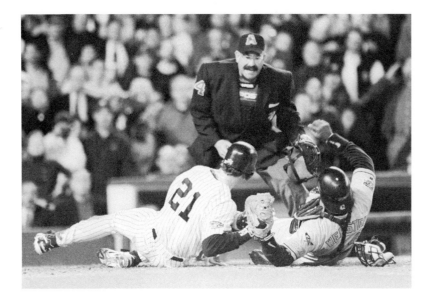

5. No decision yet by Al Clark as he waits to see the ball after a home plate collision between Paul O'Neill and Lenny Webster. (© Henny Ray Abrams/ AFP/Getty Images)

1997 OFFICIAL BATTING ORDER
(VISITING CLUB)

DATE 8/21/97

	ORIGINAL	POS.		CHANGE	ALSO ELIGIBLE
1	JETER	6	B		HAYES
			C		BUSH
2	BOGGS	5	B	HAYES	STANLEY
			C		RAINES
3	WILLIAMS	8	B		POSADA
			C		
4	MARTINEZ	3	B		
			C		
5	O'NEILL	9	B		ROGERS
			C		MENDOZA
6	STRAWBERRY	DH	B	Hayes	WELLS
			C		IRABU
7	CURTIS	7	B		GOODEN
			C		LLOYD
8	GIRARDI	2	B		STANTON
			C		BOEHRINGER
9	SANCHEZ	4	B		NELSON
			C		RIVERA
P	PETTITTE	1	B	Rivera	
			C	STANTON	
			D	NELSON	
			E		

Manager's Signature _J. Torre_

6. This Yankees lineup card from August 21, 1997, was signed by Joe Torre before it was handed to Al Clark at the pregame meeting between the managers and umpires. Note current Yankees manager Joe Girardi as the starting catcher and Hall of Famer Wade Boggs as the third baseman. (Al Clark collection)

1998 OFFICIAL BATTING ORDER
OAKLAND

DATE 6/30/98

	ORIGINAL	POS.		CHANGE	ALSO ELIGIBLE
1	HENDERSON	7	B		HINCH
			C		MITCHELL
2	ROBERTS	4	B	Boeri	VOIGT
			C		BOURNIGAL
3	GRIEVE	9	B		
			C		
4	STAIRS	(DH)	B		GROOM
			C		MOHLER
5	GIAMBI	3	B	Voigt	
			C		DOUGHERTY
6	BLOWERS	5	B		MATHEWS
			C		CONNELLY
7	MACFARLANE	2	B		FETTERS
			C		TAYLOR
8	TEJADA	6	B		
			C		
9	CHRISTENSON	8	B		
			C		ROGERS
P	HAYNES	1	B	Mathews	OQUIST
			C	Groom	CANDIOTTI
			D	Taylor	STEIN
			E	Fetters	

Manager's Signature _Art Howe_

7. Art Howe, the Oakland manager portrayed in the movie *Moneyball*, signed this 1998 lineup card before presenting it to Al Clark at home plate on June 30. Leadoff man Rickey Henderson later advanced to the Baseball Hall of Fame. (Al Clark collection)

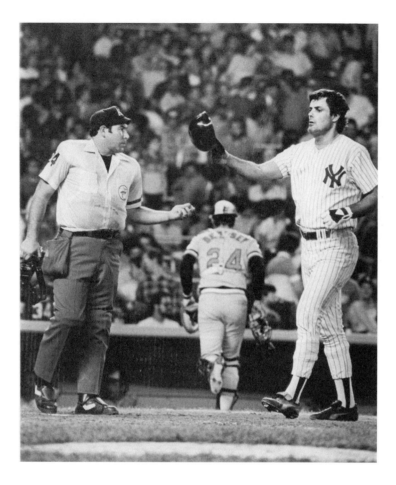

8. As Al Clark suggests, every game has three teams on the field: the home team, the visitors, and the umpires. All three are visible here: Al Clark, Baltimore catcher Rick Dempsey, and Yankees outfielder Lou Piniella. (© Louis Requena, Al Clark collection)

9. Al Clark and his younger brother Marty umpired together only once, at this spring training exhibition game in Washington DC. (Al Clark collection)

10. (*right*) Umpires were slightly less anonymous when they had their own baseball cards. (Al Clark collection)

11. (*below*) The six umpires who worked the "Earthquake" World Series were (left to right) Paul Runge, Eric Gregg, Dutch Rennert, Al Clark, Vic Voltaggio, and Richie Garcia. The photo was taken before a game at the Oakland Coliseum. (Al Clark collection)

AL CLARK 24

1989 WORLD SERIES

12. Al Clark visits with brother Jeffrey before a game at Anaheim Stadium. At upper left is cousin Lenny Balcerak. The kids, left to right, are niece Lindsey Brenner and nephews Kevin and Michael Clark. (Photo by Jerry Soifer)

13. (*above*) Al Clark (center) shares baseball memories with brothers Marty (right) and Jeff. (Al Clark collection)

14. (*opposite top*) Among the memorabilia on display in Al Clark's Virginia home is this whisk broom, encased in a shadow box to ensure preservation. Clark used the brush for twelve seasons, retiring it only after he umpired home plate in Game Three of the 1983 World Series, and calls it his most prized possession. (Photo by Dan Schlossberg)

15. (*opposite bottom*) Al Clark displays his mask and hat at home. (Photo by Dan Schlossberg)

16. Al Clark relaxes at his Williamsburg home with his faithful dog Bella.
(Photo by Dan Schlossberg)

at second, Frank Pulli at third, Steve Palermo on the left-field line and Dutch Rennert on the right-field line. After that game, umpires rotated toward home plate from first base until the conclusion of the Series.

Before Game Three, the league presidents visited our dressing room. Lee MacPhail was the American League president and Chub Feeney the National League's chief executive. I was getting ready, becoming mentally prepared, to work my first World Series game behind home plate. I was getting into the zone. Feeney walked to my dressing stall, kicked my shoes, and said, "Young fella, you've got a big assignment tonight. That pitcher for the National League, Steve Carlton, has a pitch you've probably never seen before, and you've got to be aware of it." I looked up and said, "Yeah, Chub, what's that?" And he said, "Carlton's got a great slider. You've got to be on your toes." I looked up at him again and said, "Chub, have you ever heard of a fellow named Ron Guidry? He has a pretty damn good slider, too." Chub looked down at me, turned around, and walked away. I think those were the last words that Chub Feeney and I ever exchanged.

In that game, the first player to question a pitch was Pete Rose, who pinch-hit in the ninth inning for the Phillies. I called a strike on a real good pitch on the inside corner—I'm sure Rose was looking on the outside corner. He turned around and said, "That pitch was inside." I said, "No, the pitch was a strike." He shook his head and that was the end of it. I did see him a number of years later and he reiterated that the pitch was inside. I reminded him that it was still a strike.

The Orioles wound up winning the Series in five games.

I officiated in many memorable games, from Nolan Ryan's 300th win to Randy Johnson's first no-hitter.

Remember the split season in 1981? Because of the long strike from the end of May through July, it was agreed that first-half and second-half division leaders would play off in a five-game series to advance to the ALCS. I worked the Eastern Division series between the Brewers and Yankees, and ended up working the fifth game behind the plate. Milwaukee had a marvelous team led by Robin Yount, Paul Molitor, Jim Gantner, and Gorman Thomas—he hit some long home runs. Pete Vuckovich, their top starter, was a bulldog-type pitcher and Rollie Fingers was their top relief pitcher. They didn't win the pennant in '81 but they did the next year. Led by manager Harvey Kuenn, that team became affectionately known as Harvey's Wallbangers.

Three years later, I was assigned to work the All-Star Game for the first time. Not only was I with the best players in the Major Leagues but the best players in the world, and I was thrilled to be a part of that.

The night before the game, Major League Baseball threw a lavish party at the San Francisco Opera, and as they did for all MLB parties, spared no expense. My wife, Diane, and I had taken some chocolate-covered strawberries on a plate out to the massive front steps in front of the opera house and sat down. Yankees pitcher Rich Gossage came over and asked to sit with us. He was one of the fiercest competitors ever to appear on the field but off the field was a very nice man. Here we were at the Major League Baseball All-Star Game in San Francisco, arguably one of the best cities in the country, sitting on the steps in the front of the opera house, eating chocolate-covered strawberries with one of the best relief pitchers in the history of the game. How damn cool was *that*? Gossage actually remembered meeting us when my brother Jeff asked him about it at a golf tournament years later.

It was a great feeling to walk out on the field before my first All-Star Game. At that time, the All-Star Game was just an exhibition game. It was just for bragging rights. It's no longer an exhibition because the league that wins the All-Star Game now gets home-field advantage in the World Series and has four games in its ballpark if it goes a full seven.

I have never seen a player not try to do his very best in competition on the field. That includes the All-Star Game. Even during spring training, when players are on that field, players care if they don't win. Winning is not as important as it is on Opening Day and every day of the season thereafter. The importance of winning spring training games may not be paramount, but the effort to win never escapes the Major League player.

The effort to win is magnified when a pitcher is working on a no-hitter. I'll never forget being in the house on July 4, 1983, when Dave Righetti gave George Steinbrenner a birthday thrill by pitching a no-hit game for the Yankees against the Boston Red Sox at Yankee Stadium. I was the third base umpire that day, with Steve Palermo at home, Rick Reed at first base, and Jerry Neudecker at second. But what I remember most about that day was what happened before the game.

Chuck Mangione, a Grammy Award–winning musician and devoted Yankees fan, was invited by Steinbrenner play the national anthem with his flügelhorn. Mangione and I had become friends when he started making regular trips to the Yankees spring training home site in Fort Lauderdale (before they moved to Tampa). After he learned I was working that day, he knocked on our dressing room door about an hour before he was scheduled to perform. The only umps inside were Rick Reed and myself. I introduced Mangione to Reed, and Mangione asked if he could warm up. Of course we said yes.

In the old Yankee Stadium the umpires' room was shaped like a big square with lockers in all four corners. On one of the walls was an old-fashioned Coke dispenser, the kind with the top that pulled back and forth, left and right, until someone reached in and pulled out a bottle. Mangione, as big a music person as anybody on the planet then, proceeded to lean against that Coke machine and give Reed and me a twenty-five-minute private concert. He had his hat, his long hair, and his flügelhorn, and was funkily dressed just like he was in all the posters—like Chuck Mangione. Even better, he *sounded* like Chuck Mangione.

Rick and I just sat there in awe. When Chuck finished, we laughed, we talked, and he downed a Coke. I sauntered up, took his hat right off his head, and put it on mine. I took the flügelhorn, leaned against the Coke machine, put that instrument to my lips, closed my eyes, and blew. Somehow the music I made just wasn't the same.

For me, witnessing a private pregame concert by one of America's music legends was much more memorable than the no-hit game that followed. Anybody who umpires for a long time will see several no-hitters but very few will be serenaded by a famous musician before taking the field. The fans who attended that July 4 game only remember seeing a no-hitter; to me, it was anticlimactic. It's not often anyone can say that about a no-hit game.

In one of the other no-hitters I witnessed, for example, Robin Yount of the Brewers saved the game for Juan Nieves against Baltimore by making an all-out dive to catch the last out with his body parallel to the outfield grass in right-center field. I only called balls and strikes for one hitless game in the Majors (by Randy Johnson) and one seven-inning no-hitter in the Minors (by future Major Leaguer John Denny).

I wasn't umpiring the game when Jack Morris pitched a no-hitter early in the 1984 season, but I had great respect for him as a pitcher. Morris made a difference in the era he played. My definition of a Hall of Famer is not based upon a comparison of players in different eras. But if a player made a difference in the era that he performed, then he should be in the Hall of Fame. I don't know what the writers are thinking. Morris won in Detroit, he won in Toronto, and he won in Minnesota. He won one of the most memorable World Series games ever, Game Seven of the 1991 World Series when he led the Twins past the Braves by a 1–0 score after pitching all ten innings. He won more games than any pitcher during the '80s. If that's not making a difference in the era that you played, I don't know what the hell is.

Catfish Hunter was still with the Oakland A's when he pitched a perfect game in 1968. I'm sorry I wasn't there to see it. I am grateful, though, that I called balls and strikes for Catfish later in his career. He was the best pitcher I ever saw, a real control artist. The heaviest fastball, the ball that would break the most bats, was thrown by Rich Gossage. The hardest thrower was Nolan Ryan. The *wildest* hard thrower was Randy Johnson.

There were guys I looked forward to seeing because of the baseball skills they possessed. Lou Whitaker and Alan Trammell were definitely the best double-play combination I ever saw. The best hitter I ever saw in any single year was George Brett the year he almost broke .400. Over the course of a career, the best hitters without doubt were Rod Carew, Wade Boggs, and Tony Gwynn.

The best catcher? In my opinion, people should be asking if Johnny Bench was as good as Ivan (Pudge) Rodriguez. He was the best catcher I ever saw. The best outfielder? Joe Rudi. Best leadoff hitter? That's a tossup between Rickey Henderson and Paul Molitor. The best all-around player? I've got to say two guys: Yount and Bo Jackson.

As big and hard and tough as he appeared, Mo Vaughn was soft, classy, and professional. I loved Jay Buhner's attitude. And Ken Griffey Jr. was a great kid with tremendous enthusiasm every day. Every single day. Apples don't fall far from trees. Kenny Sr. didn't have the personality of Kenny Jr., but then Kenny Sr. didn't grow up with Uncle Sparky, Uncle Pete, and all those guys on the Big Red Machine. That will give you a pretty good personality. Junior's playground was Riverfront Stadium. That was a pretty good way to grow up.

Wade Boggs and Frank Thomas were rare among hitters because they walked more than they struck out. Both of them were extremely patient at the plate. Boggs was one of the two or three best hitters I saw in my twenty-six years. He had an uncanny way of putting the bat on the ball. Rod Carew, Tony Gwynn, and Boggs could foul off good, decent pitches that they didn't want to hit until they got a pitch that they wanted to drive. I think Thomas walked as much as he did because he was so big and pitchers were a little leery of letting him extend his arms. When Thomas or Boggs got into the batter's box and I was the home plate umpire, I was aware that they had a reputation for laying off a lot of pitches. But it made no difference at all. And it shouldn't have—not to any big league umpire.

The late Yankee catcher Thurman Munson was a tremendous player. He was tenacious as hell but he had a personality that was like nails. He primarily got along with umpires, but he *really* got along with umpires if he got a hit the first and second time at bat on any given day. An umpire could pump him up by saying, "Way to go, Thurm! Man, is there anybody better than you?" He was just on top of the game. When he was behind the plate, the umpire could call a pitch right down the middle a ball and he'd say, "Aaah, get it next time." But if he went 0 for 2 or 0 for 3 and was having a tough day—or if the Yanks were having a tough day— he could be pretty tough to deal with. Munson was no different than any other catcher in the big leagues. If a pitcher let go of the ball and the catcher caught the ball without it bouncing, he wanted it called a strike. That's the way it should be. A catcher is a guy who's fighting for his pitcher, fighting for his team.

Thurman and Reggie Jackson had their differences, but both were vital to the success of the Yankees. Reggie was a great player, a Hall of Famer for sure, someone who made things happen wherever he played. He won wherever he played. That's the definition of a winner, isn't it?

There were some guys I didn't like. For example, George Bell and I just didn't see eye to eye. It was one of those personality things. In umpire parlance, one guy's prick is another's prince. Guys get along with certain guys but there are certain personalities they don't get along with.

Another guy that I didn't especially get along with—and not too many umpires did—was Tim Foli. He was just never fair. He thought anything that he did was right and anything we did was wrong. That's not the way it was. I made my mistakes, but the other guy did, too.

My rules were easy: I'll show you the respect you've earned by being there, and I expect you to do the same for me. And if you didn't, by virtue of the uniform I wore, you don't have to be there for nine innings. I will be.

Barry Bonds was not liked by the media and fans, but I'll tell you this: very seldom, if ever, did you ever see Barry Bonds give an umpire a tough time. It's not the great ballplayers that give the umpires a tough time. They don't care about the umpire. They don't care what the umpire does. They're not looking to make excuses. They're going to make things happen for themselves. They're not going to let anybody stand in the way of that job. Even in today's game, you don't see good players make excuses. Seldom do you see the good pitchers complaining. They know they're going to get guys out. They know they're that good. Good players don't care what the umpire is calling on any one particular play or particular pitch. They're thinking, "You get the next one right, and I'll strike him out with the next pitch."

Willie Wilson once had a big attitude problem. But I went out of my way to help him change. And I honestly believe that helped him become the American League batting champion.

Willie came from Summit, New Jersey, a nice suburb outside of Newark. When he got to the big leagues, he had "superstar" written all over him. I'd never seen a man go from first to third as quickly as Willie did; it seemed like his feet never touched the ground. He literally glided past second base to get to third. That's how fast and how good and how much innate moxie he had about what went on on a baseball field. He had one flaw—and it was a big one. He was a son of a bitch. He had a *terrible* attitude, especially toward umpires. Whether it was an authority thing or an umpire thing, I didn't know.

Although it was almost taboo that an umpire fly on a ball club's charter, the only way I could get from Toronto to Chicago one particular night was to fly with the Royals. The American League asked me if I would do that—they didn't make me do it—but for my own convenience I said sure and I flew with them. I also thought that was a good opportunity, since I had a captive audience.

I didn't dislike Willie and I loved his ability. So after we had taken off I went to the back of the plane, where he was sitting. It was a night flight, just a couple of hours from Toronto to Chicago. I said, "Willie, I'm going to sit down next to you for a minute, and I know you're not going to like it, but you and I are going to have a talk."

He snidely looked up and said, "What the fuck you want, man?"

I started by saying, "The main reason I'm here is because we're both from New Jersey, and there's another reason. I think it's a two-way street. You are a superstar and you're gonna be a superstar for a long time. The way to get along in this game is to get along. You can take your horseshit attitude toward umpires and jam it far up your ass.

"Let me tell you something. There's no way umpires will help you. No way, shape, or form. But umpires can sure hurt you. I'm not saying that umpires will, or that any umpire in the big leagues would make a bad call consciously or do anything detrimental to you, or any player.

"However, we are human, and if you give us a tough time, subconsciously, we're gonna be aware and on the lookout for you."

By this time—twenty or twenty-five minutes into the flight—I had his attention. I told him, "Umpires don't care if you do well or not. If you're in the big leagues or if you're not. Doesn't make a damn bit of difference to us. As long as you're going to be in the big leagues, a good idea would be to get along with umpires. How do you get along with umpires? Quite simply, don't be an asshole. Say hello. Learn the guys' names.

"You watch all the superstars, or most of the superstars. Every single game they walk out on the field, especially the older umpires, veteran players will just say hello. Quickly and quietly. Maybe as they're coming up to bat, they'll tap an umpire's shin guard with the barrel of their bat. And just say hey. Something like that. Just a professional acknowledgment.

"You're in the big leagues, you deserve to be here, and I've got respect for you. But I am, too. And you know what, Willie? That attitude will change your entire outlook on the field when you come out to play."

He didn't say very much. He was nasty. He was snide. He had a scowl on his face. Well, that was toward the end of the year. But somehow I must've gotten to him because he came to spring training with a hugely different attitude. He had decided that he was going to get along on the field.

The first time I saw him that year, maybe a month or two into the season, he came up to me and said, "Al, I thought a long time about what you said. I spoke to my wife about it. I spoke to some other people about it. And they all said you were right. That I cannot win with this attitude."

I said, "Fine. Let's see it. The proof is in the pudding. The proof is in the length of the season and your career."

That was the year he won the batting title. And he started to tell people that the reason he did it was because of the talk I had with him about his attitude. He couldn't have ever done it with the attitude he had.

I caught wind of that and saw him that winter at a golf tournament. He stood up and said, "The reason that I won the batting title was because . . ." And I said to myself, "Wait a minute. Where's he going with this?" I took him aside afterward and said, "Willie, you can't tell people that. You can't tell people that we're even halfway friends. I've got a job to do; you've got a job to do. Our jobs aren't adversarial because I'm not the enemy. The umpire is not the enemy. The enemy's in that other dugout. But there's a certain professional decorum that needs to be adhered to."

He said, "Fine." And then, when he was done with his career, and I was done with mine, he started talking about our conversation in public. Willie and I play in golf tournaments together at Sawgrass and other places during the winter and we always show a great deal of respect for each other.

George Brett, Wilson's teammate in Kansas City, never had an attitude problem. In fact he did something no other player ever did in the big leagues, as far as I know. He told every single umpire he saw that *he* was his favorite umpire. Every single umpire he came across.

Some people remember Brett for charging out of the dugout after his home run was ruled an out because he had too much pine tar on his bat. I was in the big leagues then but did not umpire that game. I can tell you, however, that the umpires discussed it and are still discussing it.

Home plate is seventeen inches wide, and there's a rule in the rulebook that says no foreign substance can be placed on the barrel on the bat more than eighteen inches up from the knob. After Brett hit a home run that put Kansas City ahead, Yankees manager Billy Martin came out to argue that he was using a doctored bat. Tim McClelland, the home plate umpire, lay the bat down on home plate, and then added an inch visually. Anything above that would make the bat illegal since the rule states that any ball struck with an illegal bat should be nullified. The batter would be called out, and all runners would return. McClelland did exactly the right thing: he called Brett out.

A protest was lodged by the Kansas City club and the president of the American League, Lee MacPhail, upheld the protest and allowed the home run to be counted. His explanation was that the pine tar had nothing to do with the lift or the distance that the ball traveled, and pine tar was not in the spirit of the rule. He did what was in the best interests of the game by thinking outside the box. Pine tar on a pitcher's hand is illegal because it can make a pitched ball sink more sharply, but pine tar on a bat is there only to help the batter get a better grip. Or so the theory goes.

I worked in Yankee Stadium many times. And I also spent a lot of time at many other famous parks. Like the vintage stadiums, the new ballparks all have their own personalities. In fact, many of them bear design elements from great ballparks of the past. I like the trees in center field in Colorado, the warehouse in Baltimore, and the cityscape in Cleveland. The Ballpark in Arlington has a little slit in right field just so a player has the opportunity to hit the ball out of the ballpark. The facilities are magnificent in every ballpark. They're baseball cathedrals. Apart from the prices, it's great to be a baseball fan in today's era and go to the ballpark to see a game.

I'm glad to see artificial turf disappearing. It was difficult on players' knees. It was also unbelievably hot in the summertime, especially in Kansas City, St. Louis, and Philadelphia. George Toma, the now-retired groundskeeper in Kansas City was also the groundskeeper for the Super Bowl for many years. He put a thermometer on the turf in Kansas City, and by the middle of the afternoon on a summer Sunday, it registered about 170.

To stand on that turf for three hours would hurt. It would start at your feet, go to your ankles, go to your calves, go to your knees, and go to your thighs. It was terribly painful. You couldn't wait to get off. It may have saved a lot of ballgames from rainouts but God still grows the best grass. What we did, between innings, was to go into one of the dugouts and stand on a three-foot-square container of ice. We'd just go and stand on the ice. It cooled down our shoes and quickly refreshed us in the couple of minutes we had between innings. It didn't do a great job, but it was better than nothing.

I had no least favorite ballpark. If it was a big league ballpark, it was a great ballpark. My adult life's work was realizing a

fantasy—every day I went to work and put on a big league uniform. My office was Yankee Stadium and Fenway Park and Comiskey Park. What a way to live your adult life. I was living a dream
and did that for twenty-six years. I don't know if it gets much
better than that.

7 Wives, Women, and Song

Unlike players, who spend half the baseball season in their team's home city, umpires are on the road from spring training through the postseason, except when they're taking vacation time. For many umpires, that regimen is not conducive to raising children or even sustaining a marriage. Maybe that's one reason I had three wives—although not at the same time—plus another marriage that lasted only one day.

Karen, my first, was nineteen when we got married. She was a beautiful young woman.

Her dad was the president of the Ewing Township Babe Ruth League and my dad was one of the coaches in the league. There was a league picnic at my future father-in-law's house. I met Karen that day. I was a few years older, but something clicked and we started going out. We fell in love, were together for five years, and married for seven, the Minor League portion of my career.

She offered tremendous support and was a wonderful young wife. But as is the case with many young couples, our interests started to differ as we matured. I was away from home for much of the year and that was difficult. Unfortunately, our youthful optimism wasn't going to last and we decided to divorce. Karen is happily remarried and I've always wished her the best.

Diane, my second wife, is still one of my best friends. I care for her and I still love her.

We met at the Newtown (Pennsylvania) Racquetball Club, where I played in the wintertime to stay in shape for the baseball season. Diane played in a league with friends after school. She was a very good looking girl who bore a strong resemblance to

Carol Burnett. I married Diane in Las Vegas, where weddings and divorce seem to happen every five minutes, and our union lasted fifteen years.

My relationship with Diane was one of huge mutual respect because we did so much growing in our thirties and forties. We put our lives together emotionally and financially. We traveled to many places in the world, from the Canadian Maritimes to the Caribbean to England, Australia, and New Zealand. We also went to many great destinations in the United States.

Our relationship ultimately failed because of the miles between us much of the year. I found it difficult to understand why Diane couldn't turn off her independent spirit when we were together. I expected her to be totally reliant on me when I was home. But the marriage wasn't going to work with those expectations.

Diane was an elementary school teacher who was in the classroom for thirty-five years before retiring. It's from Diane that I gained the respect I have for elementary school teachers, who are in one of the most underappreciated professions in our country. Teachers are charged with helping to form the ideals, the mores, and ways of our young people, as well as their attitudes. Diane did it well. She earned a great reputation as a teacher who cared. She taught me a lot about life, too.

We decided together not to have children. I chose to live my life on the road as an umpire seven months a year and didn't want to be an absentee father. I didn't feel that was the proper way to raise a family.

Since Diane is a health nut who didn't want to do anything to alter her body, I had a vasectomy. We were together during the procedure. The doctor snipped one side, looked me in the eye, and said, "Al, you've got half a chance to change your mind." Diane and I looked at each other and said, "Snip on." I have zero regrets about that decision. I think I would have been a good dad and Diane would have been a great mother. I *am* a great Uncle Al, not only to my biological nephews but to a whole host of "adopted" nieces and nephews. My friends' kids from all over the country are my most valuable assets.

I met Cynthia, my third wife, after Diane and I were divorced. I thought she was one of the most magnificent and beautiful women I had ever seen. We were introduced at Runyon's, a restaurant in Coral Springs, Florida. Cynthia was a marriage, family, and sex therapist with a thriving practice as well as a diplomate on the American Board of Sexology. How much more enamored could a good little Jewish boy be than to meet, fall in love with, and marry a beautiful sex therapist with no inhibitions?

Our courtship was a kind of whirlwind. We were married within a year or a year and a half. Cynthia and I did a lot of traveling and enjoyed a couple of very wonderful years.

I also had another wife, but only for one day.

During spring training one year, a group of friends were having lunch when we decided it would be fun to take a cruise to nowhere. There were about thirty of us on an eight-hour gambling junket. As the ship was sailing toward international waters, the captain announced that all those that wanted to get married could do so in the grand ballroom at ten o'clock in the morning. He also said that those who got married would be given a complimentary stateroom. That was all we needed to hear.

A number of us got married at sea and availed ourselves quite nicely of those complimentary staterooms. Later that afternoon, as we were leaving international waters and returning to the shores of the United States, the captain announced that anyone who chose to have their wedding vows reversed should report to the grand ballroom for an annulment ceremony. Clear thinking prevailed and there were no long-term commitments. So I was married for one day.

Over the years, I've seen and experienced many other things related to wives and women. Some of them are not printable in this book.

I umpired at an All-Star Game to which a participant brought not only his wife but his mistress, too. At one of the scheduled events, he seated his wife on one side of the room and his mistress on the other side of the room. Some juggling act! I've experienced some strange and peculiar situations in my time but never could I have even tried anything like that. I'm glad I never had to.

There's a sign in every baseball clubhouse that says,

WHAT YOU SEE HERE
WHAT YOU SAY HERE
WHAT YOU HEAR HERE
LET IT STAY HERE
WHEN YOU LEAVE HERE

I don't know the genesis of that saying but I imagine it first appeared after Jim Bouton's bestselling exposé *Ball Four*. It would be naïve to think there was never any unsavory behavior conducted on the road. But far be it for one umpire to be involved or pass judgment on another.

8 The Yiddishe Umpire

When I was growing up in New Jersey, Jewish boys became doctors, lawyers, or accountants—certainly not professional umpires. I'm proud that I was able to change that.

Because of my career choice, my name is actually the answer to two Trivial Pursuit questions, in the sports edition. One is "Who was the only person in professional sports who wore his name on his hat?" And the other is "Who was the first and only Jewish umpire in American League history?"

There have been National League umpires who were Jewish— Dolly Stark, Stan Landes, and Al Forman, to name three. Later, Paul Schreiber served in both leagues after the staffs were combined. But I was the first and only Jewish American League umpire.

People were surprised when they found out I was a Yid. They said to me, "Geez, that's not a profession for a Jewish boy, an umpire?" And they'd say umpiring is difficult and getting to the big leagues even more so, adding that if it were easy, more Jews would've tried.

I'm very proud I'm Jewish. I was bar mitzvahed in Ahavath Israel, an Orthodox synagogue in Trenton, New Jersey, in a January that had a lot of snow. I even learned to blow the shofar for the high holidays. My rabbi, Solomon Poll, took religion very seriously and was a very good teacher. Before the High Holy Days, he would bring out the shofar and show all the kids how to blow it. For some reason—maybe I was full of hot air even then—I could put the shofar on the side of my mouth and could hold the ram's horn. I could blow the shofar and make it have a true sound.

It's not easy but I didn't think it was that tough either. The rabbi took a liking to the way I could blow the shofar and assigned me to do it in synagogue during the Rosh Hashanah and Yom Kippur holidays. I was a rookie who came in cold. It's a good thing the rabbi let me take the shofar home; I did a lot of practicing. When the holidays finally arrived, I was more skittish than a cat in a room full of rockers. I was more nervous than I ever was on a baseball diamond—probably because I was so young and inexperienced. But my grandparents couldn't have been more proud. Their grandson, little Alan, was blowing the shofar on the High Holy Days. It was kind of cool.

Blowing the shofar was not only a good experience, but it also helped make me comfortable years later. I was never nervous in front of people or nervous about public speaking. And isn't public speaking supposed to be one of the most nerve-wracking things people do? By the time I walked onto a big league baseball diamond, I had years of training and experience in dealing with crowds.

I probably could have used shofar spring training but went to Yankee spring training instead. I grew up listening to Mel Allen broadcast Yankees games. We knew Mel was Jewish and came from Alabama; his real name was Mel Israel. Religion wasn't a big deal for me in the big leagues. I never forgot that I was Jewish. All I did was work hard.

With the exception of a handful of players, a few owners, and lots of writers—who wanted to be part of the game but probably weren't good enough to play—baseball is primarily a world of non-Jewish people. The fact that I am Jewish never came into play, although some people did know about it.

Some of the players today don't have a feeling of the history of the game and feel like Major League Baseball wasn't important until they arrived. They don't know the history. There are some African American players today who don't have a grasp on who Jackie Robinson was and what he did, nor Henry Aaron or Willie Mays. That's a shame. They are missing the great multiethnic history of our game.

There weren't too many Jewish players in baseball history, but the ones who were there knew who Hank Greenberg was, what he did, and how he did it. And Moe Berg. What a great story Berg's was, whether you're Jewish or not. He was a covert operative for the United States during World War II. Is there a better baseball story than a player being a spy?

One story concerning Berg and Babe Ruth is priceless. Berg was a very intelligent man. He spoke multiple languages. After the 1934 season, players took a barnstorming trip to Japan for an exhibition tour. They didn't fly in those years but took a cruise ship from Los Angeles. The Babe asked Moe if he knew Japanese. Moe indicated he did not. After arriving Ruth saw Berg speaking to their Japanese greeters in fluent Japanese. Babe approached Berg and said, "Moe, you lied to me. Two weeks ago, I asked you if you knew Japanese and you said no." Berg just looked at him and said, "Babe, that was ten days ago." On the voyage, Berg learned Japanese.

Stories like that are inherent in our history—and when I say "our history," I mean baseball history. Players today should know more about that. The history of our game is what makes it the greatest game in the world.

Later in life I realized how important Moe Berg was; I read the book *The Catcher Was a Spy*. I was proud to know that people in our game were such tremendous patriots—not only Berg but many other players who served during World War II: Ted Williams, Joe DiMaggio, Bob Feller, Hank Greenberg, and others who selflessly gave of themselves to our country. They are to be admired and honored forever.

When I was a kid I met Berg, a friend of my next-door neighbor John "Sparrow" Moran [Flip's dad]. I even remember playing catch with him in my backyard. I remember that Berg took the train with Sparrow Moran from Princeton to New York most days, and I remember he was a catcher. Moran was a conductor on the now-defunct Pennsylvania Railroad. I never met Greenberg. I know he was Jewish, and that shared bit of ethnicity made me proud Jews can excel in our national game.

Like Greenberg, Sandy Koufax retired long before I began my own baseball career. But I did meet Sandy a number of times. He is a gentleman above all, a quiet man. He gave of himself very sparingly but when he did, he was all in. He talked to pitchers whenever the situation warranted. He held nothing back once he was committed.

My Jewish pride stems from the fact that these players were as good as they were *and* we shared a heritage. Greenberg, Koufax, Al Rosen, and Ryan Braun won Most Valuable Player awards; Koufax and Steve Stone, along with half-Jew Jim Palmer, won Cy Young Awards.

Among today's players, Shawn Green carved his own niche in baseball history, hitting four home runs, a double, and a single in one game. That gave him nineteen total bases—one more than Joe Adcock, who hit four home runs and a double for the Milwaukee Braves against the Brooklyn Dodgers in the '50s. I was always a Shawn Green fan. He came to the big leagues as a Toronto Blue Jay. I knew he was Jewish and did go out of my way to be a little nice to him, to make him feel welcome to the big leagues. It was because of the kindred spirit that we all kind of have. Shawn was a good guy. After he had established himself as a star, he came to me once between innings and said, "Listen, anytime you need anything, you know, autographs or bats or balls or anything like that for any charity events, you make sure you call me first." I thought that was very nice of him. I'm glad he did well but I never would do anything to help.

There was one American League pitcher whom I will not name here. He had a very Jewish name. We were in the dugout one day before a game when he came to me and said, "Hi, Al." I said, "How you doing?" He said, "You know, it's good to see you. I hear that you're Jewish." I said, "Yeah, I am." He said, "You know, I am, too." I said, "Yeah, it's pretty obvious." He said, "I'd like to stay up in the big leagues, and any time you're back there, calling balls and strikes, would you give me a little help? I'd really appreciate it." I curtly told him that was not the way it was going to be. I also told him to rest assured that this conversation would never be repeated, not to any other umpires or to anyone else. Thank goodness baseball's umpires do not think of anything except the merits of play.

I don't think that guys knew I was Jewish. Or cared. Green knew because I told him. Rod Carew knew. Jesse Levis knew. And a few others.

There was one September game in Milwaukee when Green was batting, Levis was catching for the Brewers, and I was the home plate umpire. It was almost Rosh Hashanah. We wished each other a Happy New Year when we were together at home plate. There are so few Jews in baseball that there's a fraternity or a family that supersedes baseball. Maybe it's the heritage we've all shared. It's certainly not anything overt; it's just a feeling.

I've never been to Israel but my dad was there. He went over on a *Jewish Times* trip. He used to write for that publication, so they took him over there for a Jewish magazine convention and he had a great time.

Long after my career ended, a six-team professional league was founded in Israel. Dan Duquette, now general manager of the Baltimore Orioles, was the American contact and a number of Jewish players—Ron Blomberg, Ken Holtzman, and Art Shamsky—were involved as managers. Blomberg's team won the championship. Unfortunately, the Israel Baseball League (IBL) lasted just one season, 2007. I tried to become a consultant to that league, helping their umpires, but it never materialized. I would've loved going over and doing some clinics and working with the umpires in Israel.

I never experienced any overt anti-Semitism in the Major Leagues but had three shaky incidents back in the Minors. My partner Ted Hendry and I were walking out of the ballpark in Indianapolis after the Indians played a game against the Iowa Oaks. When Ted and I were walking to our car an hour after the ball game, there weren't a lot of people around. Denny McLain, once a thirty-game winner for the Tigers who was back in the Minors and on his way out of the game, and Ray Busse, a shortstop who had a cup of coffee in the big leagues, were both on the Iowa roster. Iowa had lost that night and I had worked home plate. Unprovoked by anything, they both started verbally attacking me: "You kike son of a bitch. What the fuck is a Jew doing in our game? You don't deserve to be here. Go the fuck home, you kike motherfucker." The players both thought their rant was quite funny, but neither Ted nor I did. It shook us up tremendously.

Ted and I went back to our hotel and called Joe Ryan, then president of the American Association. He was appalled. Ryan called the Iowa general manager and the two guys were suspended that night. When Joe Sparks, the Iowa manager, came out to home plate the next day, he couldn't have apologized more. He couldn't have been more professional. And it was certainly appreciated. I'm sure the news of that evening's after-game activity made its way around the country quite quickly.

Another anti-Semitic incident occurred in 1974, two seasons before I reached the Majors. Once again, Hendry and I were together. That time, we were sitting in a restaurant in Des Moines with former National League (and future Hall of Fame) umpire Al Barlick. He was working as an NL umpire supervisor and scout.

We were just talking, but when the conversation turned to minorities in baseball Barlick proclaimed, "I'll tell you one thing. As long as I'm alive, there will never be another fuckin' Jew umpire in my league." I looked him straight in the eye and just as boldly proclaimed, "I'm Jewish." I then excused myself, got up from the table, and left. Fortunately I never saw him again.

I felt the same way about John (Red) Davis, a career Minor League manager was running the Oklahoma City ball club during the 1975 season. We had run-ins previously but certainly nothing out of the ordinary. He voiced his displeasure with my umpiring ability. I allowed him his argument, then usually ejected him from that day's contest. No big deal. But one particular evening a call went against the Oklahoma City club. Davis stormed out of the dugout and headed right toward me. Instead of talking or yelling about the play, he said, "You're nothing but a fucking Hitler." I ejected him immediately, then walked away, leaving him to argue with no one. He finally left the field and we finished the game.

The next day, Davis said to my partner, Jerry Young, "Why did Clark run me so fast last night? All I did was call him 'a fucking Hitler.'" Young started to laugh uncontrollably, much to Davis's dismay. After regaining his composure Young told Davis I was in fact Jewish. It took Davis another two months, but eventually he did apologize and say, "That kind of shit is out of bounds."

I worked with a lot of umpires. One thing we did in clubhouses and locker rooms was tease each other unmercifully. Whether it was race, religion, politics, cleanliness, wives, nothing was off limits. With my short, squat physique, my religion, and my multiple marriages, I was an obvious target. But it was good, clean fun. However, if anyone attacked any of us outside of our clubhouse, we would circle the wagons and defend each other always. We were and are family.

I certainly wasn't the only Jewish Major Leaguer: in addition to media members and players, Bud Selig, Jerry Reinsdorf, Fred Wilpon, Bob Lurie, Ted Lerner, Jeffrey Loria, Theo Epstein, and Stan Kasten are Jews on the ownership side. Probably the most prominent Jew in baseball today is Selig, who became commissioner in 1998. Except for Judge Kenesaw Mountain Landis, he served longer in that position than anyone. But I'm not one of his fans. He did something very phony early in my career and I never trusted him after that.

Long before there was any talk of him becoming commissioner, Selig was the owner of the Milwaukee Brewers. Before a game in Milwaukee, it rained. As a result, the dugout steps were wet and slippery. I was working with Lou DiMuro. He slipped going up the steps, hit his back, and hurt himself so badly that he had to be hospitalized. An ambulance came onto the field and transported him to a local hospital. I personally went to Selig's office after the game for an update on Lou's condition and to thank him for caring. Little did I know that all he really cared about was getting Lou off the field and getting on with the game. He may have said the right words, but his actions portrayed something totally different. And ever since that happened I've been skeptical of him.

The next day nobody from the Brewers organization asked about Lou's injury or well-being. Now this wasn't necessarily Selig, but the Brewers' brass did say, "How come you guys only have three umpires today? Why didn't you bring another umpire to work?" Once again, the only time they cared about the umpires was five minutes before the game, and then they said, "Geez, where the hell are the umpires?" I never forgot that about Selig, about him not caring about Lou DiMuro.

I'm sure that as commissioner, for the game, and for the owners, he's done a good job. Some of his innovations have proven to be popular, and the newest one (the second wild card) will prove to be tremendously profitable for the owners. I'm not sure Selig did a great job for the umpires. I think he let his director of labor relations handle us. I don't know that for a fact. I don't know how much involvement he had. I do know that if he ever came into our umpires' room, it was only for a photo opportunity. He never came in and asked how our families were, never cared about us on a personal basis. And we represented him. I always thought that was kind of squirrely.

There are only a handful of Jews active anywhere in our game and only one Jewish commissioner in baseball history. I'd like to be proud of my *lantzmen* but that's not always possible. For me, that's a great disappointment.

9 Billy, Earl, and a Few Dicks

As a Major League umpire for twenty-six years, I certainly had my fair share of arguments. And, depending upon the opposing player or manager, sometimes I had *more than* my fair share. When I got to the big leagues in 1976, I encountered a handful of managers who were notorious umpire-baiters. Billy Martin, Earl Weaver, and Dick Williams were always arguing, each in his own memorable way.

Billy tried to intimidate young umpires all the time. He didn't care who you were—he tried to intimidate you if you were young. Since instant replay and slow motion on television were just coming into the picture, disagreements between managers and umpires were settled the old-fashioned way: in face-to-face confrontations. And Billy could be very confrontational. With the advent of videotape, Billy would try to intimidate the young umpires not for the call they just made but for the *next* call they might make.

Billy hardly ever got on older umpires. He wasn't necessarily arguing a particular call, always, but was looking for the inexperience of the umpire, to intimidate him, to look for the next call. If you talk to Mickey Morabito, traveling secretary for the Oakland A's, who worked with and for Billy Martin for a long time, he'll tell you that Billy was a very gracious person most of the time. He probably drank a little bit too much, but when he did a bit too much partying, he became a different character.

On the field, Billy was a fireplug. When he was a second baseman with the Yankees in the '50s, all he wanted to do was win. And he worked hard to win. You can't really fault a guy for that.

I would much rather deal with a Billy Martin, since you knew where he stood all the time, than with a Dick Williams, who was always unfair to umpires. Earl Weaver was just irascible. You knew what you got with Earl. You knew what you got with Billy. A guy like Williams was just a constant pain in the ass. Same with Frank Robinson.

Earl could best be described as an itch in the middle of your back. You just couldn't reach it. He'd go just so far and then he wouldn't go any farther. And he did it many times. He covered home plate on me one day in Baltimore. But that's just the way that he was.

Weaver was also funny. He didn't always come out with a head of steam. Once he would get going, he would be a pain in the ass. But I have to compliment him, too: he was always dynamic and in the game. He was a student of the game. He did things the Oriole Way—always being on top of the game and always working the Oriole organization's strategy, from the Minor Leagues on up.

I could care less if Earl Weaver was good, bad, won, didn't win, or was a good guy or a bad guy. But I know some of his Oriole teams were great ball clubs. He had to be part of the reason. The Earl of Baltimore did a great job as a manager. There was no strategy involved in what he did. If he was behind by a couple of runs, he waited for his power guys to hit a three-run homer for him. And in those days, during the '70s and '80s, they often did.

Earl never played in the Majors but that didn't hinder him as a manager. If you're a baseball lifer, and you spend a long time in the Minor Leagues, that is earning respect, too. If you've got the intestinal fortitude and finally get a chance in the big leagues, I think the people in the Majors have respect for you because you stuck it out for so long. They're going to give you a chance. So I don't think it's imperative to play in the Major Leagues to be a good big league manager. The current Baltimore manager, Buck Showalter, never did.

Spending his playing career in the Minors may not have bothered Earl, but his lack of stature probably did. I think Earl had an inferiority complex about his height. He was a little man, probably about 3'10". No, he was probably a little bit bigger than that, but not very much bigger than the number 4 on his back. Earl had "little man syndrome." He thought everybody was taking advantage of him all the time because of his short stature. And, of course, that wasn't the case or even close to the case. But that's what he thought for a while. And that's what we perceived anyway.

Before he retired for the first time, he said, "I am not going to let you guys kill me or give me a heart attack. I'm gonna get out of here before you guys do it to me." As if we were the enemy. He may have felt strongly that we were out to get him, but there is not an umpire anywhere who cares which team wins or loses.

He wanted people to think he stood tall in his knowledge of the rules. But Earl did not know the rulebook as well as he thought he did. Whenever a new rule was written, he would say, "I don't know about that rule, but by the end of spring training, I'll know how to get around it." So I guess he did know the rules a little. He would study a new rule and find out how to circumvent it, how to make it work for him. He didn't do it all the time, maybe just two times a season, but those two times were beneficial to him.

As an umpire, I had more respect for a guy who knew the rulebook rather than a guy who just came out to argue. If a manager came out to argue and really didn't have anything to say, he'd go on with his histrionics and yell and carry on. If he had something substantial to say, he wouldn't come out and yell. He would come out with a cool head and talk.

If I'm yelling at you, are you going to listen to me? I think I'd stand a better chance if I said, "I think I saw the play differently. Can I explain to you why I think you're wrong?" Of course you would listen—you wouldn't be bullheaded. That was how Tom Kelly, Dick Howser, and Johnny Oates handled themselves. They seldom lost their tempers. They had respect for the umpires—

and understood that they earned their way to the big leagues, too. They wanted to be treated with respect and they treated us with respect. Very seldom did Billy Martin come out and not yell with a full head of steam. Dick Williams, too. They were absolutely blustering.

Tony LaRussa, eyes bulging and neck veins straining, could argue with the best of them. But he was extremely intelligent and very fair to the umpires. LaRussa was arguably one of the better managers ever, having won almost as many games as anybody who's ever managed.

LaRussa was one of two managers (along with George "Sparky" Anderson) who won the World Series in both leagues. In the National League, he was a master of the double-switch, inserting a position player in the pitcher's spot and flip-flopping his batting order so that he didn't have to pinch-hit for his pitcher. He also tried batting his pitcher eighth, placed one of his speedsters in the ninth spot, and figured he'd create a good speed tandem if his ninth and leadoff hitters reached base back to back.

Even in the Minor Leagues, where I saw him in Wichita, LaRussa was very cerebral. He wasn't a good player but he was very smart and very observant. He had a law degree, and I often thought he was practicing oral arguments on the umpires.

LaRussa's longtime pitching coach, Dave Duncan, had a whole different approach; he was not fair to umpires at all. If his pitcher let the ball go and the catcher caught it, Duncan expected you to call a strike—as long as the uniform said St. Louis across the front, or Oakland when he was there, or Chicago when he was there. Duncan was LaRussa's lieutenant and did most of the yelling.

Like LaRussa, Gene Mauch was one of the managers who knew the rulebook well. He was also a guy who could make the rules work for him. When Mike Heath was catching for Detroit, he grabbed a loose ball with his mask. That was illegal. It was a dead-ball situation, and the runners were awarded two bases. Mauch came out and informed the umpires and he was right. That created a big brouhaha on the other side, because the other team didn't know the rule. But the umpire was right, and Mauch was right.

It's too bad that Mauch was a dour, sour man. I'm not sure that all the players who played for him respected him as much as he should have been respected. But he had a tough way to go; he had a hell of a reputation to live down from his days of managing in Philadelphia. In 1964 his team blew a six-and-a-half-game lead with twelve games to play and finished one game out of first place, behind the St. Louis Cardinals.

Mauch's reputation took another hit in 1982, when his California Angels won the first two games against the Milwaukee Brewers in a best-of-five American League Championship Series but lost the last three to blow the pennant. As an umpire in that series, I was surprised when he refused to put in Andy Hassler, a left-handed relief pitcher, to face the always-dangerous Cecil Cooper, a left-handed-hitting first baseman. Cooper came through with a big hit that drove in a couple of runs and denied Mauch the pennant.

In 1986, Mauch missed out again when the Angels blew a 2–1 lead in games and lost to the Boston Red Sox in a best-of-seven American League Championship Series. I wasn't there but I watched and was surprised when the Angels blew a three-run lead in the ninth and then lost in the eleventh inning of game five. Had they won, they would have held a commanding 3–1 lead in games.

Mauch still holds the MLB record for managing the most years (twenty-six) without ever winning a pennant.

If anybody invited second-guessing, Mauch would certainly qualify more than most. But very seldom did umpires second-guess a manager. The reason for that was we didn't like them second-guessing us.

I'm sure managers had opinions about us. And sometimes the reviews weren't very favorable. Earl Weaver, for example, didn't care who the umpire was; he hated everybody from Springstead to Luciano to Clark to Haller to Palermo to Reed—anybody you wanted to name. Earl didn't like umpires. Probably the only person who disliked umpires more than Earl Weaver was Cal Ripken Sr. He was terrible, absolutely horrible.

Dick Williams was pretty bad, too. He was one of the most sarcastic, sardonic sons of a bitch you would ever want to meet. He was as surly as anyone that I ever met in the game. I never heard him say anything nice about anybody, let alone umpires. He was disrespectful and demeaning on a personal level when he came out to argue. I don't think any umpire liked or respected him as a person. I don't even think he knew our names.

The first time I was shown up on a Major League field was by Dick Williams. He was managing the Oakland A's and I was working home plate. He didn't like the ball and strike calls I was making. He went out to talk to his pitcher. When I went out to break up the meeting, Williams looked me square in the eye, didn't say a word, and walked to second base, leaving me on the mound looking like an idiot, all by myself. And that's a pretty big show up. I said, "Dick, it's time to go. Let's go, let's play this game." He turned around and said, "I'll get off this field when I want to." And I said, "We're going to play this game." He said, "Not until I'm ready." At that point I ejected him.

Frank Robinson and I didn't get along from the first time that we met each other. It was just a personality thing. We just didn't see eye to eye about very many things, and I don't think Frank and other umpires got along very well either. No one can take away the greatness that he possessed as a player. He was a Hall of Famer for sure. There was no doubt about that. I don't know if he was a good manager or a bad manager, but I know he was really a pain in the ass to the umpires. The ironic thing is that is later, when he was no longer working for a ball club, he was hired by Major League Baseball to be one of their umpire coordinators. I thought that was pretty funny. He didn't like umpires and if he said differently, he would not be telling the whole truth and nothing but the truth. He didn't want to adhere to anything an umpire said.

I ejected Frank at home plate during the national anthem one day. That was unfortunate. It was the wrong thing to do. I should've waited until the song was over, but he really pissed me off. He was not only talking about a play that happened the day before but was doing it at a time when the managers and the umpires were standing at home plate together during the national anthem.

My partners at the time moved around and created the situation where he and I were standing next to each other instead of at opposite ends. They didn't think fireworks would go off like that but they sure did. I got a letter from the league about it, and I'm sure he did too. I was fined, and rightfully so. It was something like $500, the equivalent of a slap on the wrist.

Anytime a guy brought up yesterday's game, he was in jeopardy of being ejected. The timing wasn't much of a concern. An umpire's philosophy was this: "Let's play today's game today." If something came up, I would handle it, and I wasn't going to allow anyone to take advantage of a situation. I tried, on a personal level, to be as professional as I could possibly be. But with Robinson, I knew he didn't like me either.

Umpires react. If he was going to act like a jerk, I was going to win whatever argument we had. If he got ejected, he wasn't doing his club any good. But even if he stood in the runway, at least he was out of our hair.

For umpires, ejections were no big deal. They're part of the game, just like balls and strikes, fairs and fouls, safes and outs. When something happens and a player, coach, or manager needs to be ejected, you have an argument, eject them, and go on to finish the game. You write a report and it's out of your hands.

On the players' side, there were a lot of guys who were as difficult as some of the managers, and some who were just quirky. Albert Belle had a reputation as a hothead and a malcontent, but he did not give umpires a tough time. What a hitter he was, though. He was an enigma, a little wacky to be sure. No—a lot wacky. As a matter of fact, a lot of times, after he did what he did, and it pissed so many people off in the game, he'd look at an umpire with a wry look in his eye and a half smile. So maybe, just maybe, Albert wasn't as wacky as some thought.

But George Bell was one guy with whom I didn't see eye to eye. Again, it was a personality clash. In umpire parlance, one guy's prick is another's prince.

Another guy I didn't get along with—and not too many umpires did—was Tim Foli. He was just never fair. He thought anything he did was right and anything we did was wrong. And that's not the way that it is. Foli professed to be a born-again Christian but the language he used and actions he exhibited certainly did not reflect his alleged commitment.

Cal Ripken Jr. was a well-mannered player who was ejected only three times in his career. Most of the time, he was fine. But I was the last umpire to eject him from a game.

My philosophy was simple: I'll make my mistakes, but so will you. So don't act holier-than-thou to me. I'm going to show you the respect you've earned by being in the Major Leagues, and I expect you to do the same for me. If you don't, you don't have to be in the game for nine innings.

When I was a young umpire and Ralph Houk was the manager of the Boston club, we had a huge argument. Ralph was a former major in the marines, the epitome of old school. But he was also a tremendous baseball person. We were toe to toe and nose to nose. His head was bobbing, his hat was down on the ground, and he kicked the cap. Houk had to be ejected.

That argument happened late in the season on a Sunday. We were in Boston but just coincidentally, we were following the Boston club to Chicago for a Monday game. We got out to home plate the next day in Chicago, and, as a young umpire, I really didn't know what to expect. Was Houk going to carry on the argument? If he did, I was going to eject him again so I could earn some respect. Well, the Major came out, looked me in the eye, smiled, and said, "Young fella, we put on one hell of a show for 'em yesterday, didn't we?"

That was perfect. It was so absolutely perfect. Why couldn't every argument be like that? He had a point to get across, whether he was battling for his team or whether he thought I had made an incorrect call. But after it was over, it was over. He agreed that we should play today's game today.

Bobby Cox was ejected more than any manager in Major League history. But maybe that was because he managed for so many years. Bobby was a great old school manager, too. Like Houk, Cox was another guy who felt that today's game is today and yesterday's was yesterday. There was never any carryover. I knew Cox since he was a coach with the Yankees and later during his tenure as manager of the Toronto Blue Jays. He had that great run with the Braves, when he and general manager John Schuerholz put together fourteen straight division titles. That was unheard of and unparalleled.

Bobby Cox deserves to be in the Hall of Fame as much as Babe Ruth does. He was a baseball lifer who deserved all his accolades. Perhaps I'm talking from a stump that's a little taller and a little long of tooth, but I appreciated and respected those tough old managers very much. They were what baseball was all about.

Whitey Herzog was another old school guy. He'd give you hell. He'd come out and say, "Jesus Christ, what the hell's going on out here?" That was his favorite phrase. And he'd get into a conversation. But he was fine. There was nothing wrong with him. He was just a good old baseball guy and a good old manager who fought for his team and wanted it to be as good as it could be. What more would you want from a guy like that? He had tremendous respect for everyone in the game, no matter what level you achieved.

George "Sparky" Anderson was the epitome of a baseball lifer. Tell me when he *wasn't* in baseball. He was a great guy, a great baseball guy, and certainly a great conversationalist. He was the equivalent of a latter-day Casey Stengel. "You could look it up," as Stengel would have said. At least you could understand him most of the time. Casey you could hardly understand at all. But Sparky was a marvelous baseball man. I don't know exactly how he got the nickname Sparky but I never did call him that. I just couldn't see calling a guy who was sixty or seventy years old Sparky. I always called him George. Players who played for him, both in Cincinnati and in Detroit, had the utmost respect for him. And why shouldn't they? He was the epitome of a dedicated baseball person. He was highly successful in two cities and, like LaRussa, a world champion in both leagues.

Tommy Lasorda—there's another old school guy who was always arguing. He never yelled at a guy on a personal basis; he just wanted the Dodgers to win. I really do believe that if you put a pin in him, as he said, he would have bled Dodger blue. And what's wrong with that?

Lasorda had a great sense of humor. He once brought a hamburger out onto the field and laid it on third base for Eric Gregg, an umpire with a rather portly physique. Eric and Tommy got along fine but it was a long game and Tommy was afraid Eric was getting hungry. Maybe he was right because Eric ate it. It wasn't an argument and Tommy wasn't ejected for doing it.

Arguing with managers and players is just part of the game. There's nothing wrong with that. Every fan wants to see his home team manager come out and argue. When Lasorda came out and argued, he knew what he could say and what he couldn't say. He was a big league guy. And still is.

Some of the arguments between managers and umpires seem to take forever—but they all end eventually. When a guy is ejected, he has to leave the field or risk a bigger fine and longer suspension. The umpire can always whip out a stopwatch and say, "If you're not outta here in one minute, we're gonna forfeit the ballgame." I've never done that, but I've asked for a watch. As a matter of fact, Frank Robinson was being such a pain in the ass one day that I almost used it. And it only happened that one time. One of my partners—I think it was Chuck Merriweather—gave me the watch between innings. Most people don't know this but one of the base umpires always has a stopwatch when he's on the field. He needs it to monitor TV commercial time after every half inning. Play cannot start until television commercials are over.

So there we were, Frank and I, arguing even after I ejected him. He wouldn't leave. I was getting angrier and angrier and *he* was getting more and more pissed. So I said, "Okay, Chuck, give me the watch." Frank knew what that meant. He was going to get a time limit. Can you imagine a big league manager explaining to a general manager or an owner why he lost a ballgame by forfeit? He'd sure as hell be putting his job in jeopardy.

Forfeits do happen—think about the last game the Senators played in Washington—but they are rare. Umpires will do anything to avoid them. I've never been involved in a forfeit situation.

Frank was a great player without doubt, probably one of the best players to ever don a uniform. But he wasn't one of the better managers and I'll tell you why. Not because I didn't like him, but because very seldom do you find a superstar in our game who is a good manager. In my opinion, the superstar can't handle the fact that the players they are managing can't play as well as they did. Their expectations are way too high. Can you name Hall of Fame players who were good managers? I can name many mediocre players who were great managers. You can start with Tony LaRussa, George "Sparky" Anderson, Bobby Cox, and Tommy Lasorda.

Joe Torre was a good player but not an umpire's friend. He was very sarcastic when he came out to argue. Because he was around so long, he thought he was better than the umpires. At least that's the way he acted out on the field. He didn't do a lot to show us up except in words that only we could hear. His actions were not demonstrative, and of course we appreciated that, but his words were very cutting. I don't think anyone will look at him as a great manager, even though he managed some great Yankee teams later in his career. He didn't win in St. Louis or with the Mets, and he won a division with Atlanta, but when he got to the Yankees he was given a $200 million payroll. A whole lot of guys could win with a $200 million payroll. He was a player once, so he got along with players, if not umpires.

In 2001 Don Zimmer was my last ejection. He was the bench coach for Torre with the Yankees. He always had an air of entitlement. There was no umpire who thought Zimmer was entitled to anything. He showed zero respect for anybody who was on the field and in baseball except for the players. He would denigrate the umpires and the front office. I heard him talk about the umpires and the front office in a very derogatory way. If you weren't a player, he'd have no respect for you. And in turn there were so many people, other than the players, who had no respect for him. Especially the umpires. He was a crude, nasty, sullen, son of a bitch.

Not all arguments are alike. It fact, some of them are pretty funny. We were in Anaheim when Jim Fregosi was managing the Angels. He was a great baseball guy, best known as the man who was traded to the Mets for Nolan Ryan. Jimmy was just a good, square guy all the time.

It was the sixth or seventh inning of this particular game. I made a call that went against the Anaheim ball club. I knew I got the play right but Fregosi came flying out of the dugout. I said, "Jim, I got that play. I saw the play, and I got it right." He looked at me and said, "I don't give a good goddamn about that play." All the while, his arms are going up and down, his head is bobbing, thirty thousand people are watching, and I'm looking at him dumbfounded. I said, "But, Jim, I got the play right."

He said, "I don't care. You've been out here for six goddamn innings and haven't said hello to Preston Gomez. Preston's one of the nicest men in baseball, and I'm staying out here and not leaving until you turn around and say hello to Preston." I knew Gomez, the third base coach, had a reputation as arguably the nicest man in Major League baseball, but I was still surprised Fregosi held up the game just for that. I said, "Whoa, what do you mean, Jim?" He said, "I'm telling you, Al, I'm not leaving until you say hello to Press." So finally I turned around and looked at Preston, raised my hand halfway, and said, "Hey, Press, how you doing?" And Jimmy raised both hands, looked at me and said, "That's all I wanted." Then he turned around and went away.

Lou Piniella was fiery and feisty as a young manager but mellowed over the years. When he yelled and argued as a player or manager, he was never yelling at Al Clark personally. He was yelling because he wanted to win. When something happened that went against him and his ball club, Piniella never, in my opinion, threw anything personal out there at an umpire. He just wanted to win, and the way he wanted to win, and the way he argued with umpires, was very demonstrative.

Did we umpires appreciate that? Not for a New York second. When a guy picks up a base and throws it into right field, or covers home plate with dirt, we do not appreciate that. Absolutely not. There's a different and better way to do things. But that was his way of doing it, and, as a result, he was ejected a lot of times. But, as he got older, maybe *because* he got older, he wasn't quite as fiery. Maybe he understood a little better what umpires were about. Maybe he understood that we were working just as hard as most of his players are.

Piniella was absolutely an old school professional, as professional as anyone could get. The histrionics that he pulled as a manager, and as a player, throughout his career contributed to his reputation as a winner. As umpires, we had to understand that many of these men were Type A personalities. They wanted to win. They wanted to do whatever they could to win. We, as authoritative figures, could be an obstacle to their winning. The umpire was the guy who said, "No, you can't play anymore. Strike three. Sit down. You can't hit any more. You're out. Go back to the dugout. You can't run anymore."

When Lou was the manager in Seattle, the Mariners were in Baltimore at the end of a long road trip. They didn't play well on the trip and were looking forward to going home. Earlier in the series a game had been postponed due to rain, so a doubleheader had been scheduled. I had umpired home plate in the first game of the doubleheader and was at third base for the second game. This was in the late 1990s, when the beat writers were saying the umpires were too arrogant, had short fuses, and were too aggressive toward the players. That was really a figment of the writers' and broadcasters' imaginations because we as umpires only reacted to how the players were treating us. If a player didn't do anything or say anything to us, we didn't do anything or say anything back. But the perception was that the umpires were too aggressive.

In the game, there was a play at third base that went against Seattle. I called the Seattle runner out, and Piniella came storming out of the dugout and said, "Jesus Christ, Al." I said, "Louie, that play wasn't that close." And he said, "I don't give a damn about the play. My club is so flat that I don't know what to do." I was a veteran umpire by that time so I knew what was happening. "Louie," I said, "what do you want to do?" And he said, "I don't know, you tell me." So I said, "All right, let's just stand here and jaw. Let's bob our heads back and forth. I'll turn around, take a couple of steps. You follow me. I'll turn around again, and I'll jerk your ass." He threw up both his hands and said, "That's a great idea." So we started bobbing our heads left and right and up and down. His arms were flailing up and down and left and right. Finally I turned around and took a couple of steps. He followed me, but unfortunately a little too closely. When I turned around, he accidentally bumped me.

Lou was going to be ejected anyway, but when he bumped me, I had to eject him hard—to make it look good. Well, wouldn't you know it? One of the photographers for a tabloid called *Baseball Weekly* happened to be in the Baltimore ballpark and got some very vivid photos. When *Baseball Weekly* came out the next day, the cover showed me ejecting Piniella under the headline "Arrogant Umps." The whole thing was a setup. The media did not know what it was talking about, and when I saw Piniella again, we laughed about it.

As a rule managers argue less during spring training. Their purpose is not winning but getting ready for the regular season. I don't want to say they're more tolerant, but their focus is elsewhere. Toward the end of spring training things become a little more stringent. Even in spring training, though, there was tension when the Baltimore club was in Miami and the New York club was in Fort Lauderdale, with Earl and Billy managing. Then it might as well have been September 15, in a pennant race.

The only thing all managers had in common was that they would always get involved in arguments. If it started with a player, the manager would come out, try to intercede, and often position himself between the player and the umpire before the player could be thrown out. Players, of course, were much more valuable when they were playing rather than after they were ejected.

It was a good thing we didn't run into each other very often off the field. Umpires didn't stay at the same hotels as visiting teams. If you saw somebody you would be cordial, but you wouldn't have a beer or a sandwich with a guy. When you saw players or managers it was usually in the wintertime, at a dinner or charity golf event. Then, because we were in the same industry, there was a feeling of cordiality. But during the season, they had their job to do and we had ours. No umpire has any reason to be in the company of a manager or player during the season.

A whole new bunch of players and managers came into my life with the advent of interleague play in 1997. At first it seemed like they all wanted to test the umpires from the other league. But then I realized that because of the network of communication that exists in the big leagues, everybody knew who we were. Clubs not only keep books on umpires but there are websites with all kinds of statistics. The first time I saw that, I was taken aback.

Managers know all about the umpires who work their games. They know what they can do and what they can say. But they also need to be psychologists because players are so pampered, and make so much more money than managers, that they often have superiority complexes. That hurts their teams. I'm positive that if a guy like Mike Scioscia saw a guy not giving 100 per cent, he would do the same thing Billy Martin did to Reggie Jackson: he would take him out of the ballgame and tell him that's not acceptable. You've got to handle today's players a little bit differently than those old school managers did.

When kids grew up in the '60s and '70s, not everybody got a trophy for participating. Not everybody was told how good they were. Not everybody made the team. When you didn't make the team or get a trophy, you had to deal with it. And you probably became a better person or a better competitor because of it. Now a lot of the players feel Teflonized. They can do whatever they want, and the responsibility of their actions doesn't stick to them. Somebody will take care of it for them, be it a PR guy or somebody else in the organization. That makes life much more difficult for the manager.

10 Bucky F. Dent

In 1978, my third year in the big leagues, I received a call in Kansas City about two weeks before the end of the season from Dick Butler, supervisor of American League umpires. Butler said if there was a tie in the American League East between the Yankees and Red Sox, I was going to be one of the umpires assigned to the playoff game. The other umpires were going to be Don Denkinger, who eventually worked home plate, Jim Evans at first base, and Steve Palermo at third base. I was going to be the second base umpire.

Stevie was in his second year in the big leagues and I was in my third, but the other guys were veterans. Since there hadn't been a playoff in the American League since 1948, when the Indians and Red Sox tied for the American League crown, it was quite a feather in our caps to be selected.

It was a big, big deal and I was ecstatic, unbelievably happy. As a matter of fact, I hung up the phone, just sat on the bed, smiled, and thought, "Wow, what an honor. What a tremendous honor it was to be selected for this." And then, of course, for the next ten days or two weeks, I kept looking at the standings to see who won and who lost and whether the playoff game was going to actually happen.

I have no idea if somebody recommended me. Butler never said anything as to how we were selected, why we were selected, or anything like that. All I knew was that the four of us were picked. The selections of Denkinger and Evans, two of the stellar umpires in Major League Baseball at the time, were not surprising, but I'm sure there was a huge surprise when people heard the names Clark and Palermo. We were young, almost neophytes.

My last regular-season assignment that year was in old Tiger Stadium in Detroit. That antiquated field, at the corner of Michigan and Trumbull, was another of the great old ballparks replaced by more modern and fan-friendly parks. I didn't know if I was going to Boston that Sunday night, or back to Philadelphia and home to suburban Newtown, Pennsylvania. We were scoreboard watching. The game in Detroit, which had no bearing on the potential playoff game, was over before we knew what was going on with the Yanks or Red Sox, so I went to the airport in Detroit not knowing what flight I was going to take. When we got to the airport, we learned that the tie had in fact occurred, so I boarded a plane to Boston.

The next day, Monday, October 2, 1978, was a beautiful, cool, sun-splashed New England day. It was a great baseball day that will live in memories forever. The two great rivals—the Red Sox and the Yankees—had a long history of pennant races decided in the final game of the season. This time, the season was extended by one game, an unscheduled playoff for the American League East title.

Even the umpires were excited about it, but we couldn't share our enthusiasm with each other because we weren't staying at the same hotel. As a matter of fact Don and Steve were staying with a friend of Don's who lived in the Hub area. Jimmy was staying at a different hotel than I, and we couldn't call each other because at the time cell phones were not prevalent.

I went to the ballpark about ten o'clock in the morning. I was so enthused that I wanted to get out there and feel the atmosphere. I was sitting in the stands behind the Red Sox dugout in an empty Fenway Park when my good friend Bill White, then a Yankees broadcaster and later National League president, walked over and sat down next to me. We sat behind the dugout in a quiet, empty Fenway Park. The groundskeepers weren't even on the field. We were talking about how we'd better enjoy the quietness of the moment, because in about four hours that place was going to explode. And explode it did—with tremendous enthusiasm from both the Red Sox and Yankee fans.

In the first inning, Mickey Rivers got on base, and I absolutely knew he was going to run, if not on the first pitch then on the second or third. I was never so sure of anything on the field. Talk about being ready, being on top of your game, and knowing the situation. He was running but the Red Sox catcher made a great throw and just nipped him at second base. I saw the play. I saw it real, real well.

The turning point in the game came in the seventh inning. Bucky Dent, a shortstop not known for his power, came to bat with two men out and two Yankees on base. Dent fouled a ball off his foot, and required medical attention on the field before he could resume his at bat. Everyone in the ballpark assumed that accident would make him even less of a batting threat than usual. He had been hit pretty hard. If you haven't been hit by a baseball, by a thrown or fouled-off baseball in the Major Leagues, let me tell you this: it really hurts. You might be able to shake the pain off but it still hurts when it hits.

Dent must have shaken off the pain pretty well. Using a bat he borrowed from Rivers, another singles hitter, Dent surprised the world by hitting a pop fly into the screen above the Green Monster. That unlikely home run—just his fifth of the season—quieted not only Fenway Park but all of New England.

As the ball went out to left field I ran out toward the wall to get a better look. What a surprise when the ball left the park! Because of that home run Dent has always been known in Red Sox Nation as Bucky F. Dent.

Of course Dent's home run was not the winning blow. Reggie Jackson's home run later in the game made the difference. Lou Piniella saved the game for the Yankees by making a difficult catch in right field. He didn't make a great catch; he made a circus catch. The sun got in his eyes, he was circling under it, he happened to put his glove out, and he made the catch.

Because the game was an unscheduled tie breaker that was considered an extension of the regular season, Ron Guidry earned his twenty-fifth win against only three losses. Goose Gossage saved it for the Yankees by getting Carl Yastrzemski to pop up to Graig Nettles in foul territory near third base. Earlier in the game, Yaz had wrapped a home run around the Pesky Pole in right field so everyone in the ballpark was hoping he would do it again.

After their 5–4 victory in Fenway, the Yankees went on to beat the Kansas City Royals in the American League Championship Series and then defeated the Los Angeles Dodgers in the 1978 World Series.

Still known as "Bucky Dent Game," the sudden-death divisional playoff between the Yankees and Red Sox was a monumental, marvelous ballgame. I watch it often on ESPN Classics. I do wonder, though, who was the umpire at second base with the big mutton chops and all that hair? It was a lifetime ago, but such a great memory.

11 Labor Pains

Two men who aren't in the Baseball Hall of Fame certainly should be. They made a difference not only in the era that they served, but to baseball and to the two factions they represented. One is the late Marvin Miller, general counsel and executive director of the Major League Baseball Players Association, and the other is Richard G. Phillips, general counsel and chief negotiator of the Major League Umpires Association (MLUA) for more than twenty years.

Just as it's hard to become a player in the Major Leagues, it's tough to become an umpire. Not too many doctors or lawyers have the ability to be Major League players or umpires. The only lawyer I knew from the field level was Tony LaRussa, the longtime manager of the St. Louis Cardinals. And don't forget Dr. Bobby Brown, the former second baseman who became American League president, and Dr. Ron Taylor, a pitcher who became the Toronto Blue Jays' team physician.

Umpires don't cure cancer out there on the field, but we do the best we can with what we've got. Like players we bring special abilities to the table and deserve to be compensated fairly. That is why umpires needed to unionize.

Before 1976 the umpires were represented by John Cifelli, an attorney based in Chicago. His official title was general counsel of the Major League Umpires Association. I wouldn't say anything negative about John, because I don't know what happened before I got to the American League, but the explosion in salaries did not occur until after Richie Phillips arrived in 1978.

When Marvin Miller got player salaries spiraling upward through negotiation, the umpires were riding the coattails of those salaries. Richie Phillips proved to be the right man at the right time for the umpires. He dealt with a difficult situation and earned us gigantic gains through collective bargaining. Richie had been general counsel for the NBA referees. He made some very good gains for them. He was with that association when we contacted him. He was interviewed and hired. And for the next twenty-some-odd years he did a magnificent job.

At that time, the highest salary an umpire earned was less than $40,000 per year. That was for 170 games (including spring training). NBA officials could earn $60,000 for working fewer than 100 games.

Although the baseball umpires had a collective bargaining agreement that extended through the 1981 season, Phillips recommended that we didn't sign our 1979 contracts. Although umpires Paul Pryor and Ted Hendry had already signed individual contracts, baseball had to finish spring training and open its regular season with Pryor, Hendry, and a collection of retired, Minor League, and amateur umpires.

Until 1979, all Major League umpires were tendered separate and individual contracts. Phillips orchestrated MLB's negotiations with the association. The association would supply its members to officiate Major League games. Ironically that created the first work stoppage the umpires ever had.

We picketed in uniform outside Major League parks as fans, players, and managers grew impatient with the performance of the replacement umps, realizing the game was different without the regulars. When the labor dispute finally ended on May 15, all umpires received better salaries, pensions, per diem allowances, and more—including vacation time during the season.

The 1979 dispute was a doozy. We were out a couple of months, including spring training. I was assigned to work in Kansas City when the strike ended. There were thirty-five or forty thousand people at Royals Stadium. The fans were so glad to have the real umps back that they stood and cheered when we walked onto the field. There was no PA announcement that we were back; the fans were just aware. Knowing that applause and admiration were for us was tremendous. We really appreciated the respect we received from those fans. For once we knew how George Brett felt when he stepped onto the field in Kansas City.

Five years later we had another work stoppage. Baseball had to use replacement umps for most of the two league championship series. In fact, when Bill Deegan was brought out of retirement to umpire home plate in the American League games, he brought his old equipment out of retirement, too. As a result he became the last umpire to wear the old balloon-style chest protector in a championship series.

The work stoppages were hard. They were *damn* hard. But we all stuck together when we were earning next to nothing. Nobody wanted to lose their jobs but if we did, we weren't really losing that much monetarily because umpires weren't earning that much in 1979. That year fellows like Bill Haller and Nestor Chylak, and National League guys like Lee Weyer and John McSherry, were earning top salaries of $30,000 to $35,000 a year and per diem allowances of $55 to $57 a day to cover everything except airfare. That meant food, hotel, tips, clubhouse dues, anything and everything. It just didn't stretch.

Richie Phillips was not just good but was great for Major League umpires. He made a difference in all of our lives and the lives of future Major League umpires because of what he did and what he led us through. There were work stoppages, strikes, and some hard negotiations. Richie was involved in so many negotiations with the two league presidents, Chub Feeney and Lee MacPhail, that they actually became friendly rivals.

In 1985, for example, Richie rescued the umpires after Major League Baseball expanded the League Championship Series from a best of five to a best of seven. The Players Association had negotiated more money for those extra games in their new collective bargaining agreement but the commissioner's office refused when the umpires wanted to do the same thing.

At the time we were earning $1,500 per man for the entire playoff series, no matter how many games were involved. Phillips wanted to improve our compensation to $2,500 a man. The commissioner's office refused, saying we were in the middle of *our* collective bargaining agreement. They told Richie, "If you want more money, we'll negotiate that at the end of the CBA."

Richie kept pushing, so finally Major League Baseball decided it would submit to binding arbitration. The leagues would nominate five people, and the umpires would have right of refusal for that arbitrator. The two league presidents would have the same right to reject anyone nominated by the umpires.

The process began and the presidents led off, suggesting one of their attorneys. Not surprisingly, Richie said no. So that guy was gone. They went through eight other guys, on both sides, without agreement. All of that happened in a restaurant in New York, where Richie was meeting with the league presidents, MacPhail of the American League and Feeney of the National League. They were down to the last guy—and who knew what they were going to do?—when Richie blurted out "Richard Nixon." Feeney guffawed, threw his hands up, and started laughing. "Ha, ha, ha. Richie, if you can get Richard Nixon, you got him." All the while, MacPhail, a much more demure person than Feeney, quietly said, "Hey, Chub, wait a minute now, if Richie is saying he's got Richard Nixon, maybe we ought to think about this." And Chub, in his boisterous way, said, "No way. A former president of the United States could give a shit about umpires."

So they agreed. Little did they know that David Eisenhower and Julie Nixon (the former President's daughter and son-in-law) were next-door neighbors of Richie and Ellen Phillips in the western Philadelphia suburbs. Richie had become very good friends with Dick Nixon; Nixon was even at Richie's house for a Christmas party one year. I was there, too, and heard Nixon playing the piano and singing. Actually, the former president was quite entertaining. National League umpire Eric Gregg was there, too.

They scheduled the binding arbitration and MLB presented its case. Then the umpires presented theirs. Nixon said, "I thank you men for coming. You'll have my written findings tomorrow." Tomorrow came and the findings were revealed. Nixon said, "Baseball doesn't appreciate its umpires as much as it should. In essence, I am ruling for the umpires. However, the umpires asked for a $1,000 raise per man, and I'm not going to grant them that. Instead, in this binding arbitration, each umpire will receive $10,000 for umpiring these and future playoffs until a new CBA is negotiated."

That was a very nice development for umpires and Richie deserves the credit, not only for presenting our case but for securing Nixon as the arbitrator. Through Richie's resolve and leadership, we made huge gains that all umpires should appreciate. Every umpire should know our history just as every ballplayer should know the history of the players' association.

Richie created for us a feeling of togetherness like umpires had never enjoyed before. We made monetary and received other benefits that baseball never thought umpires would earn. If it weren't for Richie Phillips, umpires would not be earning what they're earning today. Top salaries now approach $500,000 per year. Phillips literally took the profession of umpiring out of the dark ages and showed us, Major League Baseball, and the general population of baseball fans that we are an integral part of the game. It was through his efforts in negotiating and collective bargaining that umpires began to believe not how important we were on an individual basis but how important we were to the game of baseball collectively.

The importance of experienced game officials in professional sports was proven again in 2012, when the National Football League referees were locked out. The lockout lasted about a month into the season, when complaints about officiating helped bring it to an end. The use of replacement umps proved that not everybody can officiate at the big league level. It takes training and confidence. It takes years of experience in the Minor Leagues. And it takes years of earning respect on the field from players, coaches, and managers. Just because a guy reads the Rule Book does not make him qualified. Whether the game is baseball, basketball, football, or hockey, the players are too good and too strong. The idea that anybody can officiate is absolutely 100 percent absurd. There's a certain expectation of competency at the highest level of play that just cannot be achieved by amateur officials.

Late in his tenure as head of the MLUA, Richie made one fatal mistake. It ended up costing him his job—along with the jobs of several members of the Major League Umpires Association. In 1999 our collective bargaining agreement was to expire on December 31. At the All-Star break that year, our union met in Philadelphia, which is where Phillips had his office. He wanted to talk to the membership about the upcoming CBA.

Sandy Alderson had just taken over as director of on-field operations for Major League Baseball. Alderson served as a Marine and Oakland A's executive with a reputation as a tough son of a bitch. Mickey Morabito, traveling secretary for the A's when Alderson was there, told us he wasn't a guy to screw around with. That's all we knew about him apart from seeing him stop into our dressing room to say hello before a game at the start of a series in Oakland.

Richie wanted to start negotiating a new deal before the end of the season and the end of the contract. He thought a great way to get Major League Baseball to the table would be to reveal he had letters of resignation from all the umpires that he would send to Alderson on September 1. All Richie wanted to do was start negotiating before the collective bargaining agreement expired. Nothing more. The letters of resignation were not to take effect until September 1 so there was an eight-week window after the All-Star break before the resignation scheme was to be enacted.

The threatened resignations were just a labor ploy. The theory was that MLB would not accept because it would not want to lose its umpires for the postseason. A formal, orchestrated strike would have been a wildcat strike—illegal during contract negotiations. A judge would have issued an injunction against the MLUA and we would have all had to go back to work. But if we all resigned, on an *individual* basis, that action wouldn't be deemed a strike; we were resigning.

Richie was supposed to hold the letters and tell the people at MLB that if it didn't start negotiating a new CBA by September 1, the date the resignations were supposed to become effective, the umpires would not be available to officiate during the playoffs and World Series. The problem was that instead of just *threatening* to bring those letters to New York, someone faxed those letters to the Commissioner's Office after our meeting in Philadelphia. Alderson and his attorneys accepted them and the umpires had no leg on which to stand. Sandy didn't do anything legally wrong.

Phillips made a terrible labor decision by sending those letters of resignation to Alderson. But that doesn't change my opinion that Richie Phillips was the most influential person in umpire annals ever. I absolutely believe that. He made a mistake, but who among us hasn't?

There were some umpires I'm sure Major League Baseball would have liked to release—and did by accepting their letters of resignation. There was a window for umpires to rescind their letters of resignation but no guarantee MLB would agree to reinstate them. For most, they did, but not all. Some others chose just to stay with the union and lost their jobs. Some came back later.

Fortunately for me, my first assignment after the All-Star break was in New York. My attorney, Richard Meadow, came racing down to Yankee Stadium with a letter rescinding my letter of resignation. He not only brought a letter for me but one for each of the other three umpires in my crew: Larry Young, Tim Tschida, and Rick Reed. First he said to me, "What were you thinking?" Then he told my partners, "You guys can do whatever you want with these letters but Al is signing his. I'm going to drop one off to the Major League office tomorrow, I'm going to FedEx one, and I'm going to fax one." My letter rescinding the letter of resignation was accepted. Those guys also signed theirs and sent them back. Their letters were also accepted. That's how we kept our jobs. Unfortunately, others didn't. There were sixty to seventy Major League umpires against the big corporate machine of Major League Baseball.

The whole idea of mass resignations had been suggested by one of our own in 1998. The idea came from Joe West, a free-thinking, free-spirited individual who reached the Ma124jor Leagues a few years after I did. He grew up and matured into a very good umpire and very good union leader who cares about the fellows he leads as president of the wua.

Let's face it: at the end of the day, the bottom line is it's all about money. Baseball tried to take advantage of us as best it could. Through collective bargaining, fair play, or whatever means it took through the legal system, we as umpires made tremendous gains because Richie Phillips knew the law and knew the rules. He got considerable help from the National Labor Relations Board (NLRB), which was created to protect the workers from employers' taking undue advantage of them. When the umpires had labor issues, both arbitrators and the NLRB ruled in our favor frequently.

Whenever legal issues surfaced Richie Phillips was right on top of them. He even launched a successful lawsuit against the Topps Company. Umpires were very recognizable in their baseball cards every year but were never compensated for the unauthorized use of their likenesses. Topps argued that we were public figures and didn't have to be compensated. Our lawsuit stated that because we were recognizable public figures, we should be. Richie won and we received a nice dividend. After that Topps never used umpires in its baseball cards or showed any plays in which umpires were involved.

It's too bad the legacy of Richie Phillips was tainted by the mass resignation scheme. The umpires had always stuck together. In that one situation we did not. The aftermath of the mass umpire resignation was the decommissioning of the MLUA and the commissioning of the World Umpires Association. There was much infighting about that and how it went down.

There are still some hard feelings and it's too bad, especially since those of us who were around in the mid-1970s saw the union Richie Phillips built bring us from the dark ages to a place where we were earning not only very good money but also respect in the game.

12 Quaking in My Boots

San Francisco is arguably one of the finest cities in the country, with great restaurants, wonderful theater, proximity to Northern California wine country, and great golf courses. Even when I was staying in Oakland, I always went over to San Francisco to eat and play golf.

I always enjoyed visiting the area and was honored to be one of the six umpires to work the World Series in 1989. It was the second and last time that I was selected and I was looking forward to it.

The '89 Series was played between the San Francisco Giants and Oakland Athletics, cross-Bay rivals since the A's came to California from Kansas City in 1968. Although both the Giants and A's had been in other World Series, the 1989 Fall Classic was the only one that pitted those two teams against each other. It was truly the San Francisco Bay World Series.

The A's, managed by Tony LaRussa, had Mark McGwire, Jose Canseco, Terry Steinbach, Dennis Eckersley, and Dave Stewart. Those were the stalwart guys on a great team. The Giants had Will Clark and were managed by Roger Craig. That was a star-studded San Francisco team, too.

Oakland, playing at home, won the first two games. The Series took a day off, as usual in a World Series, and went to San Francisco for Game Three.

At 5:04 p.m. PDT on October 17, 1989—a time and date that will be imbedded into my memory until the day I die—I was with National League umps Dutch Rennert and Eric Gregg and American League ump Vic Voltaggio in the umpires' dressing room in Candlestick Park when all hell broke loose.

Suddenly a roar came through that sounded like a locomotive. It was chugging and chugging and coming closer. We looked at each other and we said, "Geez, what the fuck was *that*?" The cinderblock walls in our dressing room didn't shake, as one would expect, but actually *waved*. We realized right away that it was an earthquake, which created fear along with an adrenaline rush and then panic. We knew instantly that it was powerful and thought the ballpark might fall down. We learned later that it had a magnitude of 7.2 on the Richter scale.

All three clubhouses were located under the stands at the end of the right-field foul line. The umpires' room was the first dressing room you came to after you left the field. When we realized what was happening, we bolted for the door. So we were the first ones out onto the field. I was wearing a T-shirt, long johns, and shower shoes.

We got outside in time to see the wave go through the stadium. The earth was actually moving. Candlestick Park was configured like an on-its-side S. I saw the press box and the top tier of the ballpark lunge forward and then jerk back. I saw pieces of the second deck, in the corners, fall. Then, after the shaking stopped, there was a moment when it was very calm and peaceful. Since the game was set to start at 5:30 Pacific time, the stands were not yet full. People were still arriving when the stadium started to shake.

Thank goodness the ballpark was built with what engineers call construction suspenders. The major joints were made to withstand earthquake activity and were constructed to eliminate rigidity so the structure did not collapse. When the earth was moving, those joints were designed to have a little play. Instead of crumbling, they would actually move. They did exactly what they were designed to do. No one was hurt and there was relatively little damage to Candlestick Park from the quake.

Because the people of the Bay Area and Northern California were so used to earthquakes and tremors, the fans started to applaud shortly after the shaking stopped. Their feeling was it was a cosmic sign that even though their team was down two games to none, something big was needed to get their Giants ready to win the World Series. But that euphoria lasted only a few minutes. At 5:00 in San Francisco, rush-hour traffic helicopters already in the air reported on the devastating results of the earthquake and fans in the ballpark got the news through transistor radios and portable televisions.

The ballpark was eight or ten miles from downtown San Francisco, close enough for the helicopters to see that the Mission District was on fire, a portion of the Bay Bridge had collapsed, and the Nimitz Freeway in Oakland had pancaked. All of a sudden, the feeling of euphoria had vanished. Everyone shared only one thought: "Oh, my God."

Al Michaels, who was there to broadcast the World Series for ABC, was a San Francisco–area native whose knowledge of the city enabled him to become a newsman, explained what viewers were seeing from the helicopters. He was later honored with an Emmy for his exceptional work. Michaels had been on the air doing his pregame show when the quake hit. Because the power went out he was only able to say, "We're having an earth—," but he wasn't off the air too long.

In the meantime, police cars with lights and sirens drove onto the field at Candlestick. Players milled around, looking for their wives, families, and friends.

Baseball Commissioner Fay Vincent couldn't have done a better job. Like anyone else, he wanted to gather as much information as he could before making any decisions about the future of the 1989 World Series. Since there was no power in the San Francisco area, the Mission District was on fire, and there was significant earthquake damage elsewhere in the Bay Area, Fay postponed that night's game.

We didn't know if or when the World Series would be resumed. Less than an hour after the earthquake struck, everybody knew we were in a major disaster. Fay told everybody to sit tight because the airport was closed. Some of the runways cracked, making it impossible for planes to take off or land. We were stuck in the San Francisco area for the time being, and who knew for how long?

As the days of postponement accumulated, there was a tremendous amount of pressure on Vincent to move the remainder of the World Series to a neutral site like Phoenix, or to another part of the country that had an American League and a National League team. Many options were given to him by his advisers, but he steadfastly said no to all of them. He said the people in the Bay Area had waited a long time for a Bay Area World Series, were steadfastly loyal to their teams, and that Major League Baseball was not going to deprive them of that. Baseball was going to be as loyal to the San Francisco Bay fans as the San Francisco Bay fans were to baseball. When the time is right, he said, the World Series would resume and would be a psychological boost to the San Francisco Bay Area.

That showed great foresight and made him one of the best decision-making commissioners of all time. He not only did what was in the best interests of baseball but did what was in the best interests of an entire part of the country. Fay couldn't have been more correct in not moving the World Series to a neutral spot. It gave the San Francisco Bay Area a psychological boost in the aftermath of the earthquake and the damage that it had done. Baseball was a positive force, especially when it returned to San Francisco after a ten-day postponement.

Eventually Oakland swept San Francisco in four games. But those four games took thirteen days to play. The whole experience was an odyssey I'll never forget. I had served as an umpire in the World Series only once before, in 1983, but that was tame compared to what happened in 1989.

Six umpires work each World Series, with two of them stationed along both foul lines. I never rotated to be the home plate umpire because that series only lasted four games. Had it gone past four games, I would have been at home plate for Game Five since I was at first base for Game Four. On the night the earthquake hit I was to work second base.

When the game was canceled after the quake, everybody scattered. Players, media members, and umpires all headed back to their San Francisco hotels. But I had stayed registered in Oakland. I thought it would be a whole lot easier to stay there and come over to San Francisco on the BART (Bay Area Rapid Transit). I gladly substituted the half-hour subway ride for the pain of packing and unpacking. As a result, I was the only person who was *supposed* to be on the field for that game who hadn't left Candlestick and tried to return to downtown San Francisco. The power of the earthquake scared the hell out of all of us, including me. The other umpires and I had been in earthquakes and tremors before, but none the size of that one.

After the earthquake everyone left the ballpark except for a few stadium and team employees plus security personnel. As I was walking around I saw lights and a stage that was the set for ESPN. All of a sudden it hit me: How are they telecasting when there's no electricity?

My wife, Diane, had been with me in Oakland for the first two games. Being a teacher, she left San Francisco Sunday night to get back and teach on Monday in Pennsylvania. The earthquake happened on Tuesday. She missed it. I had spoken to her on Monday, but on Tuesday, when she was watching the events in San Francisco, I couldn't call her due to electricity outages. There was no way that I could get in contact with her. As I found out later, people were calling her to ask how I was and what was going on.

When I saw that ESPN was still telecasting, I went over to one of the producers I knew and asked how they were still on the air. It turned out they had their own generator trucks. I said, "Tell you what: I'm the only person still here at the ballpark who was supposed to be on the field. I will be more than happy to go on one of your segments and talk about what happened if, after we're done, you will allow me to use one of your satellite phones to call my wife back in Pennsylvania and tell her I'm okay." He said, "Stay right here." He asked me to wait when we were chatting, left, returned in five minutes and said, "You've got a deal."

They put powder and makeup on my face and I was on air for almost half an hour talking about the earthquake, what it was like, what we were doing, and why I was there. We got done and the producer escorted me right into one of the ESPN trailers. They had cleared a satellite phone for me, and I was able to get through to Newtown, Pennsylvania, on the first try. I spoke to my wife for about ten or fifteen minutes. It was the best trade I ever made.

I couldn't get back to Oakland that night, or at least I didn't think I was going to be able to get back to Oakland that night, because a section of the Bay Bridge had gone down and was certainly closed. The San Mateo Bridge, south of the ballpark, was also closed. Because there was no electricity, BART wasn't running. There was no way I could get back across San Francisco Bay. Since I didn't have a hotel room in San Francisco, I thought I would just stay at the ballpark. What better and safer place could I find? There would be security and I'd stay in the umpires' room. It was a comfortable place. There were couches in there, along with food. I'd sleep there, and would have a much better understanding of what was happening when daylight returned.

About one o'clock in the morning the police reopened the San Mateo Bridge, which had to be inspected for damage after the earthquake. I was able to drive back to Oakland with a security guard. I went back to my hotel and was glad to find that downtown Oakland still had some electricity. The hotel was not damaged, although there was some damage in the area. I went to my room with Bob White, general manager of the hotel, and proceeded to look out the window for a while. We had a cocktail or two and talked about the evening's events into the wee hours of the morning.

After the commissioner made his decision to keep the World Series in the Bay Area, the players, coaches, and umpires were told they could go home for a few days. Since my parents and my brother lived in Phoenix, I went there to visit and wait for the series to resume.

When the people came back to Candlestick for the rescheduled Game Three, everybody was ready for the games to resume. There was a tremendous feeling in the entire Bay Area; the rivalry between A's fans and Giants fans had softened. People still wore their A's or Giants colors, but instead of being combative toward each other, they shared an air of togetherness. It was very cool and I was proud and happy to be part of it.

13 A Texas Connection

I was the home plate umpire when Nolan Ryan won his three-hundredth game while pitching for the Texas Rangers on July 31, 1990. It happened in Milwaukee County Stadium, one of the great old ballparks in American baseball history. I always enjoyed being in Milwaukee; it's a great city with great neighborhoods and a prideful population.

I had worked home plate when Nolan was pitching many times. This time I was glad to be there for a potentially historic occasion. Nolan had pitched his sixth no-hitter about a month before; he tried for his three-hundredth win a couple of times but did not earn it. When he got to Milwaukee, it was just his time to finally get over the hump.

The Rangers scored 4 in the fifth and 6 in the ninth en route to an 11–3 victory, but Nolan didn't finish the game. He had walked two and struck out eight when he turned the ball over to the bullpen with two outs in the bottom of the eighth and Texas up 5–3. Because the Rangers made three errors that night, only one of the three runs charged to Ryan was earned. The Texas victory increased his win-loss record to 11–4—not bad for July 31.

Even though Ryan pitched into the eighth inning that night, I heard that he was working out on a stationary bike when the writers got to the clubhouse. He did the postgame interviews while still pedaling to nowhere. In his twenty-fifth season in the Majors, Nolan worked terribly hard every day—especially after he pitched. He was already getting ready for his next start.

Our dressing room in Milwaukee County Stadium was adjacent to the visiting club's dressing room. After the writers finished interviewing Nolan in the Texas clubhouse, a few of them came into the umpires' room and asked me what it was like to work that game. One said, "Geez, Al. You just worked Nolan's three-hundredth win. How did that feel?" I was ready for that one and said, "Well, it was a whole lot more exciting for Nolan than it was for me." I knew getting his three-hundredth win was a monkey off Ryan's back.

Nolan had always been good to umpires. He never refused autographs, and he was always accommodating—except when he was pitching. Then he had the Jim Palmer syndrome: if he let the ball go and the catcher caught it, he thought the umpire should've called it a strike.

Since Nolan always showed the umpires respect, I thought I would present him with the lineup cards I used in his three-hundredth win. Giving something back, I think, is something we should all do, so a couple of weeks after that game in Milwaukee, I saw Nolan at Yankee Stadium. I sought him out before that day's game and I said to him, "Hey, listen, Nolan. We ask you for your time and you are great and always forthcoming. I've got something for you that nobody else can give you."

I saw him a few weeks later in Chicago and he said, "Al, I really appreciated you giving me the lineup cards. I took them home to show my wife, Ruth, and she said that was one of the nicest presents anyone could ever, or has ever, given to me. It was tremendously thoughtful." For him to mention that to me was pretty special.

Nolan was one of the best competitors one would ever see on a baseball field. He was ruthless. He would do anything to win. And if you're paying a guy like that, paying a professional athlete, wouldn't you want him to have exactly that kind of attitude? No wonder he was the first player to earn a million dollars a year.

I wasn't there when he got into an on-the-mound fight with Robin Ventura of the Chicago White Sox but I certainly remember seeing the pictures of Ryan putting a headlock on Ventura after Robin was hit by a pitch and charged the mound. When someone challenged Nolan, he wasn't going to back down in any situation. And good for him, because that's the way a professional athlete should be.

Nobody wanted to fight with him. He was a big, strong guy who could throw the ball 102 miles per hour. If you wanted to piss him off and then go up and stand in the batter's box, you were inviting trouble. Being the competitor that he was, a pitch could get away pretty easily. That was all part of the game at that time. Getting brushed back by Ryan, Goose Gossage, Randy Johnson, or J. R. Richard would certainly make a hitter think twice about digging in at home plate. They could be very intimidating.

Ryan had such a good work ethic that he pitched in the Major Leagues for twenty-seven years. No one else—pitcher or position player—has ever lasted that long.

He also did well after he retired, becoming a successful rancher and banker before buying into a Minor League franchise and later joining the current ownership of the Rangers. The team has reached the World Series twice since he became team president in 2008 and passed his philosophy of pitching down through the ranks.

Nolan retired as a player one year before the Rangers opened their new stadium, the Ballpark at Arlington, in 1994. I was lucky to be working the first game there. I umpired first base in the opening game but the Rangers lost. When I worked home plate in the second game, they won.

The next night, the night after the Rangers won their first game in the Ballpark at Arlington, I took the lineup cards out and gave them to the managing general partner, George W. Bush. It was a one-of-a-kind present to commemorate the opening of the new ballpark. Just over six months later Bush became governor of Texas.

Like Ryan, Bush had always been nice to the umpires. He was very appreciative. His wife, Laura, was there smiling with approval and couldn't have been nicer. Years later, when he was governor and on the presidential campaign trail, Richard Meadow, my New York attorney, attended a fundraiser for him. He was in the reception line to greet Bush. When he finally got to the head of the line he said, "Excuse me, Governor, I'm glad to be here, and we have a mutual friend." And Bush asked, "Is that right? Who might that be?" So he said, "Al Clark." Bush said, "You mean the umpire? Let me tell you a story." And he proceeded to tell him the story about how I came over and gave him the lineup cards. He held up the reception line for ten minutes.

George W. Bush always extended a hand, his body language was true, and his eyes were always catching our eyes. He was a first-class gentleman and probably should be the next commissioner of baseball. He loves our game and it doesn't make any difference which side of the aisle one sits on—he's a very fair man. Bush would have the best interests of the game at heart, not just the interests of the owners.

14 Lights Out in Baltimore

Randy Johnson was a very aloof individual with a very explosive fastball. To say Randy could throw the ball hard was an understatement. When he strode toward home plate with his 6'10" body, it looked like he was almost placing the ball into the catcher's glove. That's how long his stride was. He didn't necessarily throw the ball but kind of flung it. His body would be in front of his arm and then his arm would follow and he just got extra movement, extra speed out of that pitch from his motion.

He was the tallest player in baseball history and looked even bigger on the mound. He was also just wild enough to keep any hitter from digging in at the plate. Plus he had a glower that could stop a clock. He was tough to hit because of his lankiness and the way he slung the ball. Not only was his fastball Hall of Fame caliber, but his slider was, too. It made batters look ridiculous. If you were a hitter, you were easily intimidated. If you were an umpire, you hoped you didn't get hit with a pitch that the catcher missed.

Not everyone could catch Randy. Scott Bradley, still the baseball coach at Princeton University, was the catcher in Seattle when Randy threw the most bizarre no-hitter you could ever imagine. In the home game at the Kingdome he was all over the place; he not only walked six Detroit Tigers that night, but early in the game he walked the first three batters in an inning. Mariners manager Jim Lefebvre came out of the dugout and told Randy that if he gave up a run, he'd take him out of the game. So he struck out the next three guys. Boy, that was reaching, wasn't it? If one appreciates our game, and the talent that these players possess, which of course I do, then one appreciates that no-hitter was a very special performance.

Randy Johnson, like Nolan Ryan, had the potential to pitch a no-hitter on any given night. Also like Ryan, he pitched no-hitters in both leagues: one with Seattle in 1990, and at the age of forty he pitched a perfect game in Atlanta after he joined the Arizona Diamondbacks.

Randy also tried to intimidate umpires as well as hitters. He was pitching in Arizona one day when I was working home plate. He looked in at me a couple of times when he didn't like my calls. I said, "Randy, stop it, will you? Just stop it." There was no confrontation. He was the first batter in the next inning. I walked over to him and looked up—he's seven fucking feet tall and I'm five feet ten—and said, "Randy, you're looking in at me. Do you really think after all these years you're going to intimidate me?" He looked down at me and smiled, which he rarely did, and said, "No, Al, I guess not." We had no issues at all after that exchange.

Many years later I went to watch the College of William and Mary play Princeton University in Williamsburg. I was sitting in the dugout with Scott Bradley when he introduced me to his Princeton players: "This is the guy who was behind me when I caught Randy Johnson's no-hitter in Seattle." They looked at him quizzically and he said, "This is Al Clark, an American League umpire at the time." We got into a great discussion about that night—and about the great Randy Johnson—with the Princeton baseball team in the dugout at Plumeri Field.

It was not surprising to me that Randy Johnson, like Nolan Ryan, pitched well into his forties and won more than three hundred games. He was just overpowering. Batters said they couldn't see the ball. That wasn't exactly true. They just couldn't hit it. I never had a problem seeing a pitch from Nolan Ryan, Randy Johnson, or any other power pitcher. No umpire ever does.

Remember when John Kruk bailed out at home plate when facing Randy in the All-Star Game? There was an intimidation factor at work. The way Randy would sling the ball from the left side, it looked like he was going to put it right in your ear, for crying out loud. Left-handed hitters had no chance against him. The Big Unit deserved his nickname.

I was umpiring a twi-night doubleheader at Camden Yards, where Randy was scheduled to pitch the second game. The only problem was that most of the lights in the ballpark went out between games due to a nearby accident that affected a local power grid. The Baltimore power company was working on the problem but kept telling the Orioles that it was going to take another half hour. They could only turn on about 70 percent of the lights. There were at least thirty thousand people in Camden Yards who were just as impatient as the ballplayers.

I was the acting crew chief. The delay was two hours and counting when the clock read well past 10:30 p.m., but we were still hoping to start. I went back and forth between the clubhouses, trying to keep the guys informed. Lou Piniella was the Seattle manager and Davey Johnson was the Baltimore manager. Brady Anderson was scheduled to be the Baltimore leadoff hitter, Cal Ripken Jr. was involved, and Mike Mussina was the Orioles' union player representative.

It got to the point where the Mariners didn't want to play the game. They didn't want to start at eleven o'clock. They thought we should just postpone it and play two the next day. But I said, "If the Baltimore club wants to play, we are going to play."

The Orioles' front office brass wanted to play the game that night. I went into the Seattle dressing room and told Piniella that Baltimore still wanted to play. He said, "Al, that's fine. But Randy is going to be the starting pitcher, and he's already had three or four beers."

I said, "Let me go over and talk to Davey (Johnson) and the O's." I got into the Baltimore dugout area, a little bit behind the dugout in the runway. Anderson was there, Mussina was there, Ripken was there, and Davey Johnson was there, and I said, "Listen, guys. These guys say they're going to play. But I've got to tell you this. Full disclosure: Piniella said Randy is going to pitch, and he's had a couple of beers. He's still going to start."

Brady Anderson looked at me, looked at the other guys, looked at Johnson, and said, "Get me the fuck out of here. I'm not hitting against him when he's had a couple of beers." Anderson, who would have been Baltimore's first batter, was a left-handed hitter with no desire to face Johnson, a towering lefty who threw so hard that he terrorized all opposing hitters—but especially lefties. Adding a couple of beers to the equation did not sit well with Anderson or his teammates.

Since the Orioles had the option, the second ballgame was postponed.

Once the lineup cards were exchanged in the first game, the ballpark was controlled by the umpires—except in a split doubleheader. But the situation we had in Baltimore was one game after the other, a regular doubleheader—a doubleheader the way twin bills used to be played.

Once a game started, it was always up to the umpires whether it would be played without interruption. The umpires consult with the home club manager and general manager, as well as the visiting manager, and try to come to a consensus that's best suited to everyone. But there's no arbitrary rule where a power outage is concerned. There's one exception: the rulebook says the umpires must wait at least thirty minutes before a ballgame is either called or postponed. You could wait four hours. Remember in Philadelphia they stopped a ballgame at 9:00 and didn't resume it until 2:00 in the morning?

Before we had weather radar in the ballparks, the groundskeeper had to call the National Weather Service and then be put on hold for a long time. That occurred many times. The old umpire axiom regarding rain was simple: you couldn't do anything about it until it got there, and then you couldn't do anything about it until it stopped.

In today's game, you know if and when it's going to rain. You can stop the game and prepare for the inclement weather before it gets there. The umpires are told by the head groundskeeper when bad weather is coming. They have the opportunity to cover a field before it gets there, wait it out, and then uncover the field so it looks like it didn't even rain. All the ballparks today have drainage systems under the surface that can handle a deluge. If the infield is covered, the outfield is going to drain quickly—probably within ten minutes. So you're ready to go ahead and play once the grounds crew gets the tarp off the infield and takes care of any muddy areas. Then the pitchers need to warm up again.

A general rule is to play the game as scheduled if at all possible. The umpires try to be fair to everybody, visitors and home club. They make sure the pitchers have a dry mound to pitch from, the batter's box is dry, and the base paths are not too muddy. The umpires control the grounds crew and are actually in charge of the whole stadium. If it was raining, we usually didn't stop the game until the field got shiny. At that point, it was very slick. But there is all kinds of turf-absorbing compound that goes onto the field that helps absorb water.

How we dealt with bad weather always depended on the situation. The Rules Committee changed things a little bit in recent years. If the home team is not ahead going into the bottom of an inning, that inning must be completed or it's a suspended game, not a called game. In a called game, the game is over, and the score stands. A suspended game has to be picked up at the point of interruption and completed.

I think all games should be completed anyway, for the full nine innings—or more if there's a tie. The schedule calls for 162 games, so why not play all of them to their conclusion? The only time that I might agree with not playing a game to its conclusion, with one club winning and another losing, is during spring training.

During the regular season, if it's a close game, and the home team is ahead, and the visiting team has already batted in their half inning, and it's beyond four and a half innings, after the fifth inning, the home team invariably says, "How can we play in this stuff? You're going to get somebody hurt. You've got to call this game." If the situation is flipped, and the home team hasn't hit yet, the home team says, "Hey, this isn't so bad. We can play in this." And it can be the same rain. So it's up to the umpires.

Well, no, not anymore. If the home team is losing, and they haven't had an opportunity to complete their time at bat in that half inning, then the game is suspended. It is not called. If the home team is winning and the game has gone four and a half innings, the game could be called and would be an official game.

The umpires get some pressure from the general managers of the home ball clubs. They're concerned about their gate. We're talking about rain checks and a lot of money on a per-opening basis. So umpires, and especially crew chiefs, get calls from the general manager trying to pressure them into playing the game. They'll say things like, "It's not raining at the airport." And our usual answer would be, "Well, that's good it's not raining at the airport. We're not playing on runway Two-Two-Right."

Games have been postponed because of fog, wind, snow, and just plain cold weather. I can remember some very cold games in the spring and fall in Toronto when the Blue Jays played at old Exhibition Stadium. Cold is a factor in Boston, Chicago, Cleveland, and in Minneapolis again now that the Twins moved from the Metrodome to Target Field. Snow stopped a World Series in Colorado.

Umpires try to be as fair as they possibly can in any and all situations. When they ask the grounds crew to come out, they've got to come out. Planning ahead and quick thinking saves many games from being postponed, canceled, or subject to long delays.

15 The Iron Man

To be on the field in Baltimore when Cal Ripken Jr. broke Lou Gehrig's record of 2,131 consecutive games played was unlike anything else that I had experienced in baseball. There was a huge advance buildup and Major League Baseball was counting on it. A player strike had wiped out the 1994 World Series and shortened the start of the 1995 season as well. The strike situation, plus the ongoing steroids problem, had given the game a black eye. But Cal's streak represented everything positive about our game.

Being involved with a huge baseball moment is a great feeling if you are as big a fan of our game as I am. Cal Ripken Jr., who had a great work ethic from the time he was a young player in the big leagues, was as strong as anybody who ever played the game. He was revered by Oriole fans and baseball fans everywhere. His popularity was boundless. That week he could have been elected mayor of Baltimore or governor of Maryland. There wasn't anything on anybody else's mind that week except Cal Ripken and Lou Gehrig.

He worked hard to stay ahead of the curve and on top of the game by being as good as he could be, not only physically but also mentally—knowing everything that was going on, not only with the Orioles but also with the club that the Orioles were playing. He knew the opposing hitters and the strength of the outfielders' arms. Whether he was playing third base or shortstop, Cal would move to his left or right depending upon who was pitching, how he was pitching, and the tendencies of the hitter.

Cal was a master, a general on the infield. He knew exactly where to go, how to get there, and the most circuitous way to be at the right place at the right time in order to help his team do whatever it could to win. I don't mean to take anything away from anyone when I say he was one of the best competitors to ever play our game.

The only person that I think might compare with him on an everyday, day in, day out, year in, year out way could possibly be Derek Jeter of the New York Yankees. It's interesting to note that Jeter was always a Ripken fan.

I was lucky to be one of the four umpires to be assigned to the series when Cal tied and broke Lou Gehrig's consecutive games streak. Our crew (Larry Barnett, Dan Morrison, Greg Kosc, and me) actually changed our rotation on the field before we got to Baltimore so Barnett could work home plate in the record-breaking game. It wasn't difficult to figure our rotation in advance, and we realized I was supposed to work home plate. I believed that game would live in the annals of baseball forever and that the record would not even be approached. Larry, being the senior umpire on our crew and one of the senior umpires in the league, had garnered a lot of respect and deserved to be behind home plate in that game. There is honor among umpires on the field.

We went from Cleveland to Boston, then from Boston down to Baltimore. We changed our rotation in Boston so that barring a rainout, Larry would work home plate in that record-breaking game. I would switch positions with him and work second base. Kosc, who was scheduled to work first base, was a great friend of Larry's. Greg said to me, "If you're going to switch with Larry and give him that honor, why don't you and I switch, too? You work before Larry and work the game-tying game." We agreed to do that and I was very appreciative of Greg's gesture. That's how the rotation was set for the umpires to work that series in Baltimore.

Cal chatted with umpires all the time. As a gesture of friendliness or just to say hello, as he walked past the umpire the first time he came to bat, he would tap the umpire's shin guards with the barrel of his bat, nod his head, say hi, or give some other gesture of recognition. A couple of guys in the big leagues who had been around for a while also did that. It was just a show of respect, which we all appreciated.

Cal didn't say anything specific to me the night he tied the record, but he did talk to me the next night. When the game became official in the fifth inning and he broke the consecutive games record, Cal was pushed out of the dugout by Bobby Bonilla, Rafael Palmiero, and a host of others urging him to take a victory lap around the field. Nobody, especially the umpires, was going to stop him. It was literally, for baseball, a magnificent moment, a history-making event. Everyone there, including the umpires, were observing it as well as absorbing it. Even ESPN broadcaster Chris Berman, who was telecasting the game nationally, allowed the moment to speak for itself. He didn't say a word for an extended period. Sometimes silence is golden.

Camden Yards was packed with more than forty thousand people, and all became part of history. Cal wanted to acknowledge as many as he could. He lapped the field on the warning track, starting down the right-field line. He went all around the field, greeting as many fans as he could. By the time he got to third base, where I was umpiring, he looked tired.

He went over to Ron Shapiro, one of his agents, who was sitting next to the Angels dugout, shook hands with him, and then exchanged high fives and hugs from all the Angel players, who were applauding him from the top step of the California dugout. All four umpires applauded, too. That was the only time we ever applauded a player. All of us appreciated what Cal had accomplished. We celebrated his achievement not only with the people in the ballpark, and the people in Baltimore and Maryland, but with baseball fans all over the country.

It was monumental. After the game, there was a big ceremony. Joe DiMaggio was there, Cal's family was there, and all the Orioles' brass was there. While they went out on the field, I took a quick shower in the umpires' room and went up into the stands. I sat with friends and enjoyed the ceremony. Hell, I was a part of baseball history at that moment.

It was a great moment for Major League Baseball. Baseball had Cal Ripken Jr. to bring integrity and joy back to our game. The diligence, intensity, and class Cal brought to the ballpark every day cannot be denied. He was a wonderful figure for Major League Baseball.

Think about it: he played fourteen consecutive years without taking a day off. That's absolutely incredible. Can you imagine today's ballplayers even approaching something like that? Anything could've happened to snap that streak. He could've gotten hit by a pitch or line drive, or broken a finger or an arm, and gone on the disabled list. Players get hit by baseballs and get spiked all the time. He was involved with relay throws and a lot of times his back was to the play. Cal could have been taken out on double plays, sliding tag plays, or so many other situations. He was as tough as nails and never backed down from anything.

I'm sure that a whole lot of Cal's work ethic came from his dad, who was, more than anybody else, Mr. Oriole. "The Oriole Way" and "The Ripken Way" were synonymous with each other. Cal Sr.'s reputation, above all, was that of a great teacher to Minor League players.

The night Cal Jr. broke the record there was so much emotion about how good baseball was. Ripken's successful bid to become the game's new Iron Man was nothing but positive. Even though it took years to accomplish, that moment made everyone feel good again about our game. And anything that made people feel good about baseball again was just what the game needed. Cal was the show, but the even bigger show, in abstract, was the good feeling that baseball had that night.

Before the "2131" game, I walked downstairs with my friend Woody Woolwine and heard a guy yell, "Woody!" I looked over and saw Bruce Hornsby, a Grammy Award winner, and Winton Marcellus. They were going to do the National Anthem that night. They came over to talk to us. I said, "If you need to warm up, come by our dressing room." And Hornsby said, "You got a piano in there?" That reminded me of the game at Yankee Stadium when Chuck Mangione came into the umpires' dressing room to warm up. Luckily for us, he brought his own flügelhorn. Musical instruments are not common sights in umpire dressing rooms.

I remember everything about that night, even the little conversations I had with Cal during the game. I was working third base. Between innings I would move over behind the shortstop position like most third base umpires will do. It was nothing special. We just let it flow. We knew what was going to happen and were glad it didn't rain.

Cal's home run against Shawn Boskie in the fourth inning was almost anticlimactic in retrospect. The players, fans, and media were waiting for the fifth, when the game became official and Cal's name replaced Lou Gehrig's in the record book. He must have felt relieved that the long marathon was over. As the Baltimore fans celebrated, Cal showed his relief and appreciation by running around the diamond. The game was stopped for twenty-two minutes.

When Cal ran that lap, it was a lap of celebration for Cal. It was a lap of celebration for all of baseball, still smarting from the 232-day labor dispute that ended a few months earlier. All of us in the game felt that Cal's timing couldn't have been better. That moment was bigger than umpiring, bigger than any one individual. Like all the Cal fans, I was a baseball fan. I was a fan of our game, and our game was enjoying a joyous moment, a resurgence. I loved it. I'll always remember the date: September 6, 1995.

To this day Cal is very respectful of the game and the people in the game. But he is not as perfect as the public perceives him to be. He's great with the media guys, great when the red light of television is on, but he also has what I call the superstar syndrome. Certain guys are so far above superstar status that if you happen to be in their company and you're agreeing with everything they say, they'll allow you to stay there and talk with them. But as soon as you disagree, they will blow you off in a New York minute.

Cal was ejected only three times in his Major League career. I was the third umpire to eject him. The other two umpires to eject him were Drew Coble and Tim Welke.

For me it was a real simple ejection. It was a hot Sunday afternoon. The Baltimore club was going to take a three-and-a-half-hour flight to Texas after the game. I was behind home plate. The streak was still intact, and—this is all conjecture on my part—he probably would've liked to have taken a couple of innings off. In the second inning Cal looked at a third strike and took exception to being called out. He knew exactly what to say to me, as the umpire behind home plate, to get ejected. Cal put on quite a tirade. Davey Johnson, the manager at Baltimore then, was standing there aghast as Cal went through his histrionics before he left the field.

He later admitted he was wrong. Cal actually apologized to me on television that evening. I saw it. And, for him, mission accomplished. The streak was still intact and he had time to get some work on his body before the plane ride to Dallas.

16 Credit Denied

My career as a Major League umpire ended because of something I did after an extra-inning game in Atlanta.

Thanks to collective bargaining, Major League umpires flew first class when going from assignment to assignment. I was assigned to travel from Atlanta to Boston with a day off between games. Umpires were allowed to downgrade those first-class tickets to coach if we were deviating from our travel schedule on an off day to go home. That's exactly what I had done.

I owned a home in Boca Raton. I was going down to the West Palm Beach airport to spend a day off in Florida, then fly coach up to Boston from West Palm Beach. I had downgraded the ticket legally, from Atlanta to West Palm, and then was flying coach again from West Palm Beach up to Boston.

My wife was with me in Atlanta. And the game in Atlanta went into extra innings. I missed my scheduled flight from Atlanta to West Palm Beach. There was only one more flight that evening. I had to take it or stay in Atlanta. On that flight, however, there were only first-class seats available.

I did not have my personal credit card with me to pay for the upgrade. But since I was coming from the ballpark, I did have in my pocket my League-issued Universal Air Travel card, a credit card for plane travel. I used that to upgrade both my wife and myself so we could get to South Florida on the last available flight.

My career-ending error was neglecting to call the commissioner's office the next day and tell what I had done; I also used the air travel card not only to upgrade myself, but also to upgrade my wife. I should have sent a check for the difference. Incidentally, the day after the off day, I did fly coach from West Palm Beach to Boston for my assignment. When I was called into the office a number of weeks later, they asked me if I had done this and I readily admitted it. I completely forgot to call. And that's why I was terminated. I felt being fired was much too harsh. The penalty didn't fit the crime. Perhaps a fine or even a suspension would have been justified. But termination was too tough after twenty-five years of loyal service.

Baseball would much rather have their umpires travel as a crew, be a unit, fly together, and stay in the same hotels. I was never of that mindset. I was never afraid to go by myself. I was never afraid to be independent. And that ultimately is the major reason for my downfall. It was not over memorabilia. That didn't happen until after I was terminated.

After being terminated, I went into retirement only a year and a half earlier than I had planned. An umpire's severance package in 2001, after twenty years of Major League service, called for a one-time, $400,000 payout, along with pension and major medical benefits. Baseball did not want to pay me the severance package, but through negotiation I earned a $250,000 payout. My other earned benefits are still intact today.

I admit I felt a great shock at losing my job. There was a tremendous amount of shame involved in just being fired. But I sought and received therapy, which helped. I wasn't the first guy to lose a good-paying job and career inside or outside baseball. I always lived by the edict that baseball wasn't the end, but was always only a means to an end. The end was being in retirement and enjoying the fruits of my thirty years on the road. I love living in Williamsburg, Virginia. I sit on my back deck and watch golfers go by.

But I couldn't help but think that others in the game have done a whole lot more wrong, outside the realm of legality, who got second and third chances—not only umpires but players, coaches, and managers. Should they get a second chance? I'm not sure.

I'm not the person to ask because I didn't get a second chance. But to be fired for that?

I'm also reasonably sure that my later legal troubles, the ones that resulted in my incarceration, wouldn't have happened if my career as an umpire hadn't been cut short. This is all speculation on my part for sure. One thing I'm sure about is this: I believe I was treated unjustly by the people in the commissioner's office.

Sandy Alderson, who is now general manager of the New York Mets, was then the vice president in charge of on-the-field activities in baseball, which included umpiring. Ralph Nelson was supervisor of umpires. Ralph didn't like me and neither did Frank Pulli, a former umpire who was also a supervisor at the time. They didn't appreciate the fact that I was as independent as I was, and that was unfortunate. But I wasn't going to change. They wanted everybody to act primarily the same way, just like all the NBA referees and all the NFL referees. Everybody was supposed to make calls the same way. There was not supposed to be a whole lot of personality displayed by the officials. I didn't agree with that at all; I think officials who show some personality add something to the game.

When the credit-card issue happened, I was fifty-three years old. All I wanted to do was complete the 2001 season, work one more year, and then retire after my fifty-sixth birthday the following January. Had everything happened as planned, I would have umpired twenty-seven years in the Major Leagues—a fine career by any standard. I don't know if Sandy Alderson was aware of my plans and I don't believe he cared.

Our union, the World Umpires Association, went to bat for me, but Major League Baseball had made up its mind. I was an employee. I was tired and about ready to retire anyway. I had a great career. I had a wonderful career. What happened happened.

Bigger people than I have been fired from bigger and better jobs than mine—for probably lesser reasons. My life is not going to be defined by the fact that I was fired by Major League Baseball. My life will be defined by how I reacted to adversity, and how I've always treated other people. And helped people.

I can look in the mirror. If I had my druthers, would I have preferred not to have been fired? Hell, yes. Would I have preferred to retire from baseball when I was ready, as I had planned? Absolutely. But it didn't happen. I accepted what happened, tried to understand why it happened, learned from the experience, turned the page, and moved on.

Were there any long-term ramifications? I don't know if I was blacklisted by anybody, but I must admit there were occasions when I tried to get back into baseball. I never was able to get past a first phone call.

I would have enjoyed being a Minor League observer of umpires. I would have been a good evaluator. Not a supervisor, but a scout. Like a Minor League scout for umpires. I live in a very good area for that. Not far from my Virginia home in Norfolk are the Peninsula Tides, and Richmond, home of the Flying Squirrels. With thirty years of experience under my belt, I would have loved to have gone and observed umpires, made reports on them, and been part of the process of helping the umpire profession. That never happened. When other retired umpires suggested similar ideas, it *did* happen—even though they were not necessarily in such proximity to Minor League ballparks as I was. I think I might have been blacklisted, although I've got absolutely no proof of that whatsoever.

I always wondered why Major League clubs don't hire umpires as either scouts or coaches. We see the players up close and personal. And we see the pitchers from sixty feet away. When a pinch hitter comes up, we can see whether he's so aggressive that he's trying to squeeze the sawdust out of the bat or coming to the plate with his head down and shoulders slumped. The second is defeated before the umpire says, "Play ball." I can tell probably 90 percent of the time if a guy's going to be successful. As Yogi Berra said, you can learn a lot just by watching.

If organized baseball didn't want to take advantage of my experience, it was their loss. It was obvious to me the commissioner's office didn't appreciate my attitude; I can tell when I'm getting the cold shoulder. Baseball wanted people to fall in line and do things their way. They wanted everybody to stay together. I don't think they liked the fact that I was independent and created other opportunities for myself because of baseball.

Probably the best example of my independence was my public relations company, Ump's Eye View, an enterprise that involved such companies as Polaroid, IBM, and US Air Freight. Ump's Eye View was a public relations company that my partner and friend Red McGarry and I founded. I originated the name and he incorporated it. I came to be friends with Red through a mutual friend, Harry Toussant. Red was a marketing guru for the 3M Corporation who lived in St. Paul, Minnesota. When we found out we were both New Jersey natives, that was the beginning of a great partnership.

Our families also became very close. In fact, his daughter Laurie invited me to speak when her fifth-grade class had show and tell. I went in with all my umpiring equipment and passed it around to all the students. During the question-and-answer session, one of the kids asked me about a Minnesota player. Without thinking about the audience, I told the kids, "He's a good fuckin' player." All the youngsters reported to their parents that someone in class used the "F word." That was my only appearance at Laurie's school.

Some words you just wish you could take back. Fortunately for me, that stay in Minneapolis was only three days and I was gone. But I stayed in touch with Red and his family.

Red was a marketing genius who hatched the idea that we should host corporate representatives and their clients before ballgames. We put our plan together and hired other umpires, too. We would meet our guests at the press gate about an hour and a half before the ballgame, escort them to the seats that were given to the umpires, and sit with them for up to a half an hour, talking with them about their home team, umpiring, and baseball in general.

The whole concept promoted our national game to people all over the country. And our clients appreciated it. We would follow up the next day with either a phone call or a visit to the people we had seen the previous evening. All the while, we were promoting the game. It was a real positive, win-win situation for baseball.

It was a win for the company representative because he spent time with a customer outside the workplace. It was a win for the customer because he and his family enjoyed quality time together at the ballpark. Our seats were usually located behind home plate. It was a perfect family outing.

Major League Baseball didn't take too kindly to our activity, and they viewed it as a conflict of interest. Although it lasted ten years and was a tremendous marketing tool for the game, baseball officials put a stop to it. The only explanation, or so it seemed at the time, was that they wanted a percentage of our fee. But no one from the commissioner's office ever came out and said that.

Major League Baseball then changed the rules regarding umpires' hosting others before games they were working. It ruled that umpires going to the ballpark had to go directly to the dressing room. We couldn't sit in the stands. We couldn't earn any money outside of umpiring during the season. In the off-season, there was no problem with our doing virtually anything we chose. After the season we seldom heard from the commissioner's office until the beginning of the next year. We were just done.

17 Jailhouse Rock

When life throws you a curve, you make the best of it. You do what you think is right, without hurting yourself or anybody else. I struck out and paid a heavy price for that mistake.

After having the privilege of wearing a Major League umpire's uniform for twenty-six seasons, it was quite a shock to find myself dressed in prison garb just three years after I left the big leagues. There was no way in hell I should ever have spent a minute in the Big House. Yet there I was.

The source of the whole situation was not actually what I did, but what I was *accused* of doing. I was accused of authenticating balls from David Wells's 1998 perfect game at Yankee Stadium. I did not officiate at that game and did not sign any letters of authentication from it. Richard Graessle, whom I had met a few years earlier, admitted to forging my name and saying that the balls were given to me by one of the umpires who officiated in the perfect game. That lie launched the investigation into me and the memorabilia situation.

The problem started when I was still an active umpire in the late '90s. I met Graessle through a friend, Dave Harmon. Dave and his wife, Chris, were good friends, and Graessle was a collector and memorabilia salesman who drove a delivery truck in New York City.

Graessle came down to Trenton to see Dave at Logo 7, his place of business, several times a month or whenever he needed or wanted something from Dave. I met him during the off-season. He seemed like a good guy and became a friend. I enjoyed meeting his family and gave some baseballs and pictures to his kids.

I gave those things to his family because I thought they would like them. There wasn't really a whole lot he could do for me. But he was a good guy and I became involved with him. I just didn't see the depth of deception in Richard's dealings with people. I had no idea whatsoever.

He asked me to do a couple of things, such as authenticating baseballs from games I was in, but sometimes there was more authentication than actual game merchandise. I thought I was just doing a nice thing—not necessarily a good deed—as I had done so many times with so many people around the country. I never took a single dime or charged him for anything.

My last salary was about $375,000 a year. I never took any money from Graessle because any money that he could have given me certainly would not have changed my life and wouldn't make a difference to me: I was doing something for a friend. I never thought it was that big a deal until it became a big deal.

My problems started when I signed some letters authenticating balls supposedly used in Nolan Ryan's three-hundredth win, a game in which I was the home-plate umpire. I may have given him four or five baseballs but probably signed fifteen letters. I just didn't think it was that big a deal. It wasn't illegal to do that but it was morally wrong. What got me into trouble with the law was the fact that some of those letters of authenticity I signed in Williamsburg and put into the U.S. mail constituted mail fraud. That was the federal crime; I pleaded guilty to one count of mail fraud.

I had been thoroughly investigated by both the FBI and the Internal Revenue Service. My attorney, David Fassett, and I had multiple meetings with both agencies. I told them everything. I was forthright and forthcoming with them in every single meeting. They scrutinized every bank account I ever had and every trip I ever made but found no evidence of any extra money coming into my accounts. The reason they found no extra money coming into my accounts was because there was nothing coming into my accounts from Rich Graessle or anything I did with him. I never accepted a dime. That was proven by the fact that the judge, the FBI, and the IRS never found that I took any money. When Graessle was sentenced, however, he was fined at least $100,000 for back taxes and avoiding income tax. That didn't happen to me. I had to make restitution; the judge made me pay $40,000 to the Baseball Assistance Team (BAT), a charity that helps indigent former players, umpires, and others from the baseball family. I was also sentenced to 120 days of incarceration in the low-security camp section of the Petersburg Federal Correctional Facility.

The prosecutor and my attorney had made a deal that I would serve no jail time but would do a lot of community service and perhaps pay a fine. From what I understand, 90 percent of the cases when a federal prosecutor and a defendant agree on a plea, the judge rubber-stamps it and goes on to the next case. But my judge, John Bissell, wouldn't accept it. He said in open court that I was a public figure who had violated the trust of the public and therefore he was going to make an example of me. When he said that, my attorney's shoulders slumped, his head went down, he turned to me, and under his breath he said, "We're in trouble." The judge explained that once I agreed to plead guilty on one count of mail fraud, there was no appeal. Whatever punishment he meted out was the punishment I would receive. The only way I could have appealed would have been if I had had a trial by jury. With that, he proceeded to sentence me to four months of confinement.

The judge was a former hockey referee and sports fan who said in open court that he respected my work. He's retired now but was a federal judge then in the Newark District in New Jersey.

After the court proceedings, which lasted two days, the judge asked me if I wanted to say anything. I said yes. I had written a page-long speech about how ashamed I was, how I'd made a mistake, how we all sometimes make mistakes and how sorry I was for my family, my friends, Major League Baseball, and baseball in general. It was quite heartfelt and I meant every single word of it. There was nothing to hide at that point. No punches to be pulled. I made a mistake. I admitted to it from day one.

I guarantee you there are a whole lot of people in a whole lot of communities, people in business, who have done much more immoral or illegal things than I did. But I got caught. I believe that it wouldn't have been quite as bad for me if I wasn't a semi-public person, having spent twenty-six years in the big leagues. I was also known and respected in the New York area. When I was sentenced, for thirty-six hours the scroll across the bottom of ESPN's *SportsCenter* carried the news that I was going to be incarcerated. Every newspaper in the country reported it. It was terribly embarrassing.

After the news became public I received calls, notes, letters, and e-mails from many, many umpires. They were people I lived with, people I worked with, people who were partners, and people who were just members of the staff. Only one person in the administration of baseball called and that was Mickey Morabito, traveling secretary of the Oakland A's. He had broken into baseball as a batboy for the Yankees and was a great friend to all umpires. He called to offer support. But, other than my fellow umpires, no one else in baseball ever did.

I had a four-month window between the time I was sentenced, in February 2004, and the time I had to report. When I walked around my community, went to the golf clubhouses and the restaurants, I heard whispers. People would say, "Hey, there's Al Clark. He's going to jail." That didn't deter me from doing what I wanted to do and being where I wanted to be. I knew what kind of person I was. People who knew me knew what kind of person I was. I couldn't do anything about people who didn't know me or people who wanted to form opinions because of something they read, and wasn't going to try.

As the time drew closer for me to actually "go away" my anxiety and fear grew greater and greater. Nobody I knew at that time had been incarcerated. Since then I've found out that a lot of my friends have admitted to me that they had been incarcerated, too—for anything from driving under the influence to some kind of fraud. People I never thought would be involved in that situation were. These were good friends of mine whom I just didn't know about.

I know it's out there but I'm willing to talk about it. I'm willing to put myself out there. I've never been afraid to put myself out there. Mickey Mantle was taken advantage of by many people in business situations because he wasn't afraid to take chances and put himself out there. I put myself out there, too, but somebody cut off the branch I was standing on and I paid the price.

I had to get used to the idea that I was going into a situation that I never thought would involve me. During the pretrial hearings, I had to report to a woman in Norfolk a number of times. One day she said, "Listen, Al, I've gotten to know you and I have to tell you this: not everybody who goes to jail is a bad person or criminal. People who go to jail have made mistakes. And this will not define who you are. This is just a facet of your life."

That facet started in the summer of 2004 when I reported to the federal prison camp in Petersburg. It was not like checking in to a Four Seasons, believe me. The legal system can send you anywhere, to any federal facility. They could've sent me to Seattle. I requested that I serve my sentence in Virginia, in Petersburg. Based on the fact that they had room, that request was granted. So that's where I was assigned.

They gave me some clothes, they took my valuables, and I gave them some money so that I could buy things at the commissary (it was available once a week for a couple of hours). Then they marched me to another building away from the administration building. They put me in a room where a doctor gave me a physical. Shortly after that, the camp administrator came in, asked the doctor to leave, and said, "Sit down, relax." I did sit but was not very relaxed.

She introduced herself as Debra Gonzalez-Kozier, former director of the camp at Fort Dix Federal System. There were no female prisoners in the camp—they had a separate facility. The director was in the system for a while and was obviously good at her job. The administrator said she knew all about my case. She also said I was going to be categorized as a celebrity inmate and told me not to tell anybody what I did, not to tell anybody where I came from, and certainly not tell anybody how much money I had earned. Then she added, "Do yourself a favor and mind your own business. You're not going to be here that long and these people will find out soon enough who you are." That was the best advice I received.

When we got done with that and some other administrative stuff, I was taken to a dormitory, a couple of stories high, and was placed in a lower bunk bed outside one of the guard's offices. (Climbing up and down from an upper bunk would have been tough in the wake of my hip replacement.) I stayed there for three of the four months that I was incarcerated.

I was sitting on the lower part of a bunk bed when a guy came up to me and said, "You're the fucking umpire, aren't you?" I hadn't been in the facility more than two to three hours and hadn't spoken to anybody other than the doctor and the administrator. I looked up at him and realized I was in a quandary. I didn't know whether to lie to him or tell him the truth, what to say, or what not to say. I was just given advice by the camp administrator to not talk to anybody, not tell anybody what I did. But I figured I was going to be there for four months. So I said yes, I was the umpire. That got around the camp within three or four hours; Al Clark—they even knew my name—was in the Petersburg federal camp.

These guys were all baseball fans and liked sports in general. That's how they filled some of their idle hours. They all had radios and listened to their favorite teams' games. So they wanted to talk to me and wanted to know what was going on.

The quasi-celebrity status was kind of beneficial because many of my fellow inmates had done much worse things than I did. Most were drug users, drug pushers, pimps, or robbers. There were very few violent criminals because you couldn't be in the low-security camp setting if you had more than ten years, or 120 months, to serve.

I had situations go on inside that were harrowing or tough, but some that were funny.

We could move around. There was a track. There was a work-out area. There was a basketball court. There was a football field. There was a commissary that was open a couple of hours one day a week. There was a bunk area. There were no walls around the facility. There were guards who constantly patrolled the area. You could literally walk out any time. But if you got caught, you would be placed behind bars. Once or twice while I was there, somebody left but we never saw him again because he didn't come back to the camp. You could be booted out of the camp and into a lockup facility if you were caught with any contraband: booze, drugs, or even cell phones. Believe me, I did none of that. I wanted to do my four months and get out.

While I was there I did make some friends—or at least incarceration friends. There was one fellow whose nickname was T. He never really held a job and had been in and out of the legal system for thirty-five of his fifty years. He was a pusher, a user, a pimp, and a thief from the Washington DC area. He commanded a tremendous amount of respect from a lot of the younger inmates from the DC area.

Somehow T and I became good pals. He was my best friend while I was incarcerated. He helped me and taught me a lot about the system. He would say things like, "Not all closed eyes are sleeping." In other words, you've got to be aware of what's going on around you 24/7. For my first three months, I bunked with T. We had adjacent beds in an open area. That was how we got to know each other. It was like the middle of a dormitory building that had a ground floor with nothing in it except bunk beds. There was no privacy.

There was one television room, where the most powerful people decided what to watch. There was always a lot of sports on, for example. That was hardly a lounge-type situation. It consisted of an open floor where the guys sat on folding chairs. After you were there for a while, you got a chair and put your number on the back.

I was there about three weeks before I got a chair, but two weeks after that, the chair was stolen. I was sitting on my bed one afternoon when T returned from his warehouse job. When he noticed the downcast look on my face he asked, "What's the matter?" I said, "Nothing." He said, "Don't you motherfucking lie to me. What's the matter?" And I said, "Man, somebody stole my chair." He said, "You stay here a minute."

Now you've got to understand that if you are incarcerated, time means nothing. When an inmate says, "I'll see you in a minute," that minute might be sixty seconds, sixty minutes, sixty hours, sixty days. It means nothing. It's just a word. Well, this gentleman said, "I'll see you in a minute."

By that time, another guy came over and said, "What's going on?" I said, "Somebody stole my chair and T's going to find it." He said, "Man, that's not good." I said, "What do you mean?" He said, "Well, he's gonna create something." I said, "What do you mean he's gonna 'create' something?" He said, "You know. He might be going to create a family reunion." I looked at him quizzically and asked, "What are you talking about?" He explained, "When are the only times families get together? Weddings and funerals. And there ain't no weddings in here."

About forty minutes later, T came back with my chair. I asked him, "Where'd you get the chair?" He said, "Don't ask no questions." I asked, "Who had it?" He said, "I told you, don't ask no fucking questions." I said, "Well, T, where did it come from? Tell me something." He said, "Shut the fuck up. You got your chair, that's it." That was the last that we spoke of the chair and no one ever touched my chair again. You don't think that's scary?

I later formed a very peculiar odd couple with Frank Taylor, a big, nasty badass from North Carolina. He had been there for years and was going to be released about the same time I was. Nobody could handle rooming with him or bunking with him. One of the lead guards asked me if I would mind bunking with Frank. I didn't have any problem with that at all. He was of some interest to me because he was an absolute loner. No one talked to him. I had tried to talk to him, just by saying hello.

Frank was strong, black, bearded, and intimidating looking, but extremely clean. He would mop his floor every day. Married to a minister, he was down for thirteen and a half years. He had been rehabilitated. He knew what it would take to be on the outside and was determined not to come back to prison or endure any more incarceration. He was an intriguing figure, about six feet six, and very hard. When they asked me, I said, "Let me talk to him first." I went up to him and said, "You've got a month left, I've got a month left. How about if you and I do the time together?" He asked, "Why are you even asking me?" I said, "Because they asked me to ask you and I don't have a problem bunking with you. You never treated me poorly and I always treat a guy like he treats me. Reputations don't mean a damn thing to me. I don't care how big you are, how bad you are, or how tough you are. You never did anything to me."

He asked if I was afraid he *might* do something to me and I said no. He looked me in the eye, I looked him in the eye, and I said, "I would be more inclined to be frightened if you didn't have the balls to look at me in the eye." He said, "C'mon, move in, we'll get along fine." For the last month, we got along with no problem at all. Others couldn't understand how two complete opposites—a little fat white guy and a big tough black guy— could get along as well as we did.

Among the inmates, nobody talked to each other. Everybody yelled. And everybody yelled over each other. So there was always a constant, great din of voices and noise. Just noise. It wasn't like fifty thousand people roaring at a ballpark. But it was a constant, constant noise. For seventeen hours a day there was a constant buzz. There was very little respect for others who were also incarcerated. Everyone was self-absorbed, concerned with what they were doing and how they were doing it. The people who talked the most usually had the least to say. Inside the dormitory building, there was nothing to absorb sound—just cinderblock and metal. There were no curtains or fabric or anything. Empty barrels made the most noise.

One particular day, a couple of months into my stay, this one bombastic bastard was bothering me. He was loud every single day. We were inside the building and fifteen to twenty yards from each other. I was not having a particularly good day and was feeling some anxiety, maybe feeling a little sorry for myself. I heard his voice and that's all I could fucking hear. So I turned around and said, "Gonzalez, why don't you shut the fuck up?" I did it in my boisterous umpire-type voice, and with that, about two hundred other inmates who were on the first and second floor got quite quiet. And I asked myself, "What the fuck did you do?" I was fifty-four years old and that guy was thirty-five, in great shape, young, aggressive, and angry.

He looked at me and yelled across the room, "You fat motherfucker. You want a motherfucking piece of me?" Well, I had to do something. I couldn't back down. I was going to get my ass kicked, but I was gonna get a shot in first. I didn't answer his question directly. I said, "Just shut the fuck up." By that time, a whole crowd of people was watching from the second floor, leaning over the railing. A path had cleared between him and me. It was like a play, when commands from the director have people make way so a fight can occur. He started coming at me and yelling, "You want a piece of my motherfucking ass? You're gonna have it, you're gonna get it right now." And he kept on coming. I don't know if the adrenaline in my body has ever been that high. But I *couldn't* back down. I *wouldn't* back down.

If I was going to get my ass kicked, I was going to get my ass kicked. But I was going to get a shot in first. When he got about ten yards from me, I assumed a fighting position. Fists clenched, body turned, I was waiting to be attacked. He was being aggressive, and I was trying to be as aggressive as my shaking body would allow. He closed to about five yards from me, all the while yelling at me, and I was saying, "Come on. Come on, motherfucker." All of a sudden he blinked. He stopped. He pointed his finger, and he said, "You better stay the fuck out of my way." And I said to him, in a not-so-loud voice, "Just quiet the fuck down." He turned around and nothing more was said. But nobody else fucked with me the rest of the time there.

There were no fights because the consequences were too great. Once you were involved in a fight, you took the privilege of being in the camp away from yourself and were sent back to a general population where there were bars and cells. You had to go along and get along and mind your own business. There were many cliques—based on color, religion, or something as simple as how long your hair was. People hung together. I minded my own business for my four months.

Inmates' daily conversations every day focused on drugs, what legal work could be done to have their sentences shortened or overturned, and the prison facilities they had been in previously. They talked about drug programs and halfway houses but never about families, job prospects, previous occupations, education, or educational prospects.

A high point of every day was mail call. Everyone congregated around the guard distributing the mail. Inmates were not allowed to handle any mail at all, but I helped unload the bags and separate periodicals from mail so guards could distribute them.

Unfortunately many guards in the system were not real smart. We had a female guard who could barely read. She was distributing mail and there was a letter for a guy whose first name was Charles. I handed her the letter, she looked at the address, and said, "Char-les, Char-les." No one responded. She looked at me, and I looked at it and said, "Charles." At that point she looked at it and said "Charles" and the guy's last name. That's how sad these people were. It's a good thing the guards in the prison camp were not given guns. They were there more for show and control.

We had a head count five times a day. One count was always in the middle of the night. One was at bedtime, one was when you woke up in the morning, one was in the middle of the afternoon, and one was after dinner. Two of them were stand-ups, where somebody would come around with a clipboard and a roster. We had to check off our name; show our ID, which we had to have with us at all times; and recite our personal federal prison number. If those three things didn't match, something was wrong. Or if they got done with the count and somebody was missing, there was a total lockdown. Nobody could leave the bunk area. Everybody had to come back, no matter where they were in the camp, until the missing person was found.

As inmates we had to comply with all kinds of rules, covering everything from the clothing we wore to telephone etiquette and visitors. We all wore blue shirts, khaki pants, and steel-pointed shoes. Everybody was allotted three hundred minutes per month on the telephone. You had a fifteen-minute limit per call and there was always a forty-five-minute wait before you could use the phone. Every phone call in and every phone call out was monitored. The numbers you call had to be cleared and you could receive a call only if the caller's number had been cleared.

Visitors also had to be investigated and approved before they came in. No visitors who weren't on your visitors list were allowed. Each inmate had to sit facing forward. There was no touching or very little touching: one embrace in, one embrace out, and neither for very long. Kids could not sit on an inmate's lap. The guards were afraid of any kind of contraband transfer. The last five guys out of the visitors' area every day had to be strip-searched. Everyone coming in was patted down; everyone going out was patted down. We could put ten people on our visitors list; my visitors list included my wife, my two brothers, my dad, and a couple of friends. Neither my dad nor my brothers came.

My dad was very disappointed when I was sentenced. He said to me, and I'll never forget this, "How could you?" and "What were you thinking?" I said, "Dad, I just never thought it was gonna be a big deal." He said, "Well, I guess you were wrong." And that was it. I had already been terminated from baseball, so going to jail and being incarcerated didn't cost me my job.

Because my dad and one of my brothers lived in Arizona, visiting me in a Virginia correctional facility would have been hard for them. It was much easier for my wife, Cynthia, and a couple of friends who lived in Williamsburg. So those three were the only people I saw from the outside, except for a rabbi who volunteered his time.

Cynthia came twice a week, and my friends Mike Mitchell and Al Klapperish came with her a few times. Al was one of the builders of my Williamsburg house who went out on his own and became a handyman. A navy veteran, he could fix anything with his hands. He didn't necessarily do it quickly, but he did it accurately. He used my house in Williamsburg as his office, worked in Ford's Colony as a handyman, and was busy all the time. He had access to my checkbook and to my house and was a great and trusted friend. Mike was a native New Yorker who later lived with me in Williamsburg.

Conjugal visits were not allowed. We visited with family and friends in a big room with chairs. And there were rules with the chairs. You had to sit forward, facing a certain area. You couldn't sit facing each other. There were guards there who would let you know in no uncertain terms if you violated the rules. They didn't care if they embarrassed you. Guests also had to be dressed appropriately. No revealing clothes could be worn by women or men.

Since I didn't have too many visitors, I was glad to get a lot of mail from friends and family. The guards opened every piece of incoming mail and had the option of opening every piece that went out. We would get mail in envelopes that were opened or stapled shut after being opened.

I received anywhere between six and ten letters every single day. That's a lot of letters to receive in 120 days. But it kept me going for much of the day: reading letters, rereading letters, writing letters. While you're incarcerated your biggest enemy is idle hours. If you don't fill the time with something to occupy your mind intelligently, the idle hours can be your biggest enemy. I did an awful lot of reading and writing. I did a lot of letter writing. I kept a journal, too.

Everybody had a job in jail unless he had a medical problem. Since I had a hip replacement and also had an abscess on my toe that created a bone spur, I couldn't wear steel-toed shoes. That was ironic since I wore steel-toed shoes every fourth day for thirty years in baseball. In prison, guys needed them for protection in case something dropped on their feet.

I only worked four hours a day because of these problems. My job was to dust off the top of a desk, dust off the frame of a picture, and dust off a bannister. That job paid seventy-nine cents a day and was supposed to take four hours. Needless to say I took a lot of breaks. I had a rag, the only piece of apparatus I needed for that very intense job. It was the same bannister every day, same picture frame, same desktop. Some might call it busy work but others might say it was quite substantial. During my breaks I read, I went outside to smoke, or I just hid. Nobody was watching Al Clark. The guards were looking for something that was going awry. As long as I did my job and nobody was bitching and complaining about me, the guards didn't care.

Since I had so much time on my hands, I walked a lot and lifted weights a little bit. I walked up to eight or ten miles every single day around the track and football field. I wound up losing more than fifty pounds. But I also got a little stir-crazy. After a while I said to myself, "I'm a prolific golfer. I enjoy playing golf all the time. Why don't I go to the recreation director and ask him for a pitching wedge and a couple of golf balls? I could spend my time honing my skill with a wedge."

I thought that was a pretty good idea. I presented it to the recreational director and he agreed. He said, "Al, that'd be a great idea. Except there's only one problem." I said, "What's that?" He said, "Someone is going to take that golf club, knock off the wedge part of it, make it into a spear, and then we've got problems." That was the extent of my golf experience; I didn't play for four months.

I had better luck turning my Major League umpiring career into a practical prison pastime. After I showed some of the inmates how to catch and throw a baseball, one of the decent guards asked me if I would do an umpire clinic for guys who wanted to be umpires. I said, "Sure, I'll be more than happy to do not only an on-the-field clinic, but also a rulebook clinic." I was not only to do the basics, like balls and strikes and safes and outs, but to show guys how to position themselves. So for two weeks, three days a week, for most of the time I was there, I held an umpiring clinic. Each one lasted about an hour and a half.

We had classroom sessions and we went out on the prison's ballfield. While other guys were playing a softball game, I had my class of umpires out on the field, teaching them the right way to officiate a baseball game. We talked about positioning, talked about how to call a ball, a strike, or an out. We went out on the field and I placed runners around the bases, showing those guys where the umpires should be to better control the game. The participants of my umpiring class and clinic umpired the camp softball games; it was a win-win for everybody.

About twenty-five guys signed up for the class. They got extra credit, which meant some decent perks like being first in line to eat. If you're locked up for a long time, eating first is a big deal. At the end of the two weeks, all of my guys got certificates. They were computer-generated and supplied by the prison. The head guard signed them, I signed them, and the guys put them in their jackets or in their personal folders. If that's not turning a negative into a positive, I don't know what is. I could authenticate every one of them.

I never officiated at their games because their season had just ended. I saw a couple of their games, though, and talked baseball with the guys. We talked about their favorite teams and their favorite players. They watched baseball on television all the time. Since Washington did not have a team then, most of them were Oriole or Yankee fans, so when they played each other, as they always do at the end of the season, there was some controversy—not only on a close call but also when an Oriole or a Yankee did something good. There was a lot of cheering and raucous behavior to show up the other guys.

The camp had baseball, basketball, and football. Everybody tried to cheat so nobody could officiate. They called their own fouls in basketball, which if you watched was hilarious. Just imagine these guys when they started arguing about whether it was a foul or wasn't a foul.

There were plenty of arguments but usually the umpire won. Sometimes, however, the gang mentality prevailed. Players would scream at officials, "Are you *sure* you want that man to be out?" Or they would threaten, "I'll kill you if you don't call me safe." When they couldn't resolve disputes, they would have do-overs, just like kids do.

There should have been do-overs for the food. It was really horrible. I couldn't imagine the food being any worse. But as bad as the food was, there was tremendous waste. Every night they would throw away cases of food. Big loaves of bread. Bologna.

Dozens of eggs. I spoke to the director of food services and said, "We're not too far from Richmond. Surely there are homeless shelters, institutions, or food banks that would be willing to come and pick up the food you are throwing away." Their answer was "It ain't gonna happen because it's government issued and, once it's government issued, it has to be used in the way that's intended or it gets disposed of." How fucking stupid was that—especially when there are people who are homeless and hungry? If it was good enough for a prisoner, wasn't it good enough for anybody else? Talk about tax dollars being wasted.

We had access to a microwave so that we could cook whatever you could buy from the commissary, like cans of soup. We certainly weren't served steaks, chops, or chicken. The inmates loved to make their own food, especially pizzas. The guys would get tortilla shells and cut up tomatoes and cheese. They were quite ingenious and actually came up with some great dishes. You know, necessity is the mother of invention. It was good to have friends who could cook—or at least know how to use the microwave pretty well.

We weren't supposed to take anything out of the kitchen. Nor were we supposed to cut in line at the mess hall, since that showed disrespect for everyone else. If you were caught and were considered unintimidating, you would be sent to the back of the line. If you *were* intimidating, the guards looked the other way. There was a caste system for sure. The inmates in the kitchen crew stole food all the time. Then they would barter for whatever they needed or wanted when they got back to the dormitory.

There was some thievery going on in the camp and some gambling, too. They took away our valuables when we reported but guys had cigarettes, shoelaces, and other things of value in that situation. And we needed them.

Among the camp population of about 450 men there were carpenters and electricians. A bunch of them said they could make prefab homes, box them up, warehouse them, put them on a truck, and take them to whoever needed them most after a natural disaster like Hurricane Katrina. But then we figured it couldn't happen because it was too intelligent and cost-efficient but not wasteful. Those were *our* answers as to why it couldn't be done.

There were lots of unforgettable characters in the camp. We had an investment banker nicknamed Johnny Goody-Two-Shoes. He wasn't a bad guy. But he created a fraudulent situation involving millions of dollars in international currencies. He had a son and daughter he loved very much and was quite remorseful about being in the camp. He was an intelligent guy who taught high school equivalency degree classes for the other inmates.

Another guy, Dave, from outside Philadelphia, was a kind and soft man who loved the Jersey shore. He drove a bus for the camp while he was there. I don't know why he was there but it couldn't have been for anything violent.

Another fellow was down for twenty-two years. When we talked about it—and this struck me as very odd—he said, "I've only got six and a half more years to go." *Only* six and a half more years? That was quite strange. He was a jailhouse cook who was very institutionalized. He could do most anything with a microwave.

Another fellow, Turek, from New York, loved the Yankees and listened to their games every day on the radio. If anyone said anything nasty about the Yankees, it was like a bull seeing red. He'd get angry and would want to fight.

We even had a father and son serving at the same time. They had been in the drug business together.

Inmates talked about their time in terms of months. Nobody said they had ten more years; they would say "120 months." Psychologically, months didn't seem as long as years.

One of the main topics of conversation was Inmate.com. The guys would talk about it as if it were an actual website. It wasn't. It was a rumor mill filled with misinformation. It was nothing serious, but the rumors ran rampant.

To relieve the boredom, the camp occasionally showed movies. I'll never forget watching *Escape from Alcatraz* there; some
of the inmates thought they were watching an instructional film.

I didn't experience any anti-Semitism, but I don't think the
other inmates knew I was Jewish. They would have if they had
read my file because I wrote "Hebrew" when I had to indicate
my religion on a personnel form. There was one other Jewish guy
in there and a rabbi would come and see us once a week. We sat
with him for an hour and talked about whatever we wanted to
talk about: Judaism, anxiety, leaning on faith, anything. It was a
way to feel your faith in a faithless situation.

During the High Holy Days, the rabbi came and we participated in a short service. The rabbi wasn't allowed to bring us
anything but did manage to bring in some prayer books. The
prison even created kosher meals for us. We sat in a room, just
the three of us, and talked about the holidays. One time we talked about when and how we were bar mitzvahed, about some of
the High Holy Days that we had experienced in the past, and
about Judaism in general and what being Jewish meant to us. It
was cathartic, in a way, because it was an escape hatch for our
minds. At that time we felt we really were not incarcerated, that
our minds were allowing us to free ourselves from where we were.
That, of course, was quite important.

For a lot of people in prison, God was not a savior but a com-
panion, a friend, and a confidant—someone for people to talk
with. Through observation, I saw their belief as a soothing, calm-
ing entity. A lot of inmates read the Bible. I thought it was strange
that God and the Bible were encouraged for people who were
incarcerated, but banned from our schools and courtrooms. I
don't quite understand that.

I didn't understand quite a few of the things I saw and heard
in Petersburg.

One day I saw three young African American guys sitting in
the cafeteria. I was sitting there minding my own business and

listening to these three twenty-year-olds who knew each other on the outside. The first one said to the other two, "Man, what you guys doin' today?" And the second guy said, "Man, I gots to go to the till." Then the third guy said, "Man, what times you got to go to the till?" The second guy looked at him and said, "I gots to go to the till right after lunch." The first guy looks at him with a strange expression and said, "You gots to go to the till? Man, what the fuck's the till?" The other two looked at him, and the second guy said, "Man, you know. The hos-pi-till." I about fell off my stool. It was hilarious.

One guy was talking about another inmate and talking about how long he had been there. He had not been there very long. He said, "Man, he ain't seen nothing. He's only been here two years. He's still shittin' Burger King."

I was watching a poker game one day when one of the guys came out with a saying that broke up the whole group. One of the guys made a move with his cards and one of the others said, "You're holding those cards longer than they held the hostages in Iran."

Just by observing, I realized that the inmates were not there to be punished; they were there as punishment for what they did. Time was measured differently there. Outside the gates, there was Eastern time, Central time, and Pacific time, but inside there was also CPT. The inmates called it Colored People Time. They just went about their business in their own timeframe. They could do whatever they wanted as long as they didn't break the rules.

The whole place was the best form of socialism anyone could imagine: three hots and a cot. Everyone was treated the same. They got three hot meals a day, heat in the winter, and air conditioning in the summer. They had no responsibilities and they couldn't go anywhere.

The complex had counselors but they were very difficult to talk with. One of them told me the only thing that made him mad was when people talked about politics, religion, or anything else.

Prisoners might or might not have known humility before they came to Petersburg but once there, they learned to be humble. I found out so many things while I was there. I found out whom to trust, whom not to trust, whom to talk to, whom not to talk to, what to do, what not to do, when to do it, and when not to do it. The longer I was there, the more familiar I became with my surroundings and what I could or couldn't do. I'd become involved with the daily life of the camp.

The situation was bad and the memories are tough, but I absolutely believe in turning a negative into a positive if I possibly can. I think I did that. I hoped that anybody that I cared for—family, friends, associates—would only learn and feel that experience vicariously through me. It's a terrible thing to have your freedom taken away.

I never spent one hour in a cell in the four months that I was incarcerated. But there were limits to where I could go. Just the mere fact that I couldn't go beyond a line gave me the feeling that I'd lost my freedom.

I learned that idle hours can be a tremendous enemy. One has to occupy one's mind, whether by reading, writing, thinking, or walking. One has to look himself in the mirror and come up with solutions to the problems that are being flung around in one's own mind. I did a lot of thinking, introspection, wondering, and writing during my four months of incarceration.

The irony of being in jail was that time was standing still in my life. Nothing was going forward, nothing was going backward. But time kept passing. Even though I was stagnating by being there, someday the bit would be over. Thank goodness time kept moving.

I started counting the days and hours until my release only in my last month. I learned a couple of things I had not known before I was incarcerated. I learned a different level of patience. I learned that time is just time. It doesn't go fast, nor does it go slow. Time is just constant. With that comes the understanding of patience. I was a much more patient and tolerant person coming out of being incarcerated than I was before being incarcerated.

I'm a positive person. If I can create a positive situation from a very negative one and put a spin on it that not only works for me, but someone else also can take advantage of my misfortune, that's a very positive thing. Instead of lamenting over the hardness of being incarcerated, I wanted to find out if there was anything that was positive about it.

Inmates told me over and over again that they didn't want to wait for their last day in to prepare for their first day out. If they didn't want to come back, they had to prepare themselves while they were inside to do something productive on the outside. The prevailing sentiment was this: "One of these days, and it won't be long, you're going to wake up and I'll be gone."

I was supposed to be released at 7:00 in the morning. A couple of days before that I saw the guy who comes to sign inmates out. I said, "Miguel, listen. I'm getting out of here on November 10. Please get here on time that day. Don't make me wait." And he said, "Mr. Clark, I will be here as soon as they open the doors at 7:00." And he was there at 7:00. I didn't even stay for breakfast. I walked over to the administration building with this guy. There was a process to being released. Part of that process was giving back the prison clothes, putting on the clothes I came in with, and collecting the money that was in my prison bank account.

My civilian clothes were too baggy but I didn't care. That was of no concern. My wife was there, she picked me up, and we left. I never looked back. The first thing I did when I got out was to kiss my wife. The facility was about an hour and a half from home so we stopped at a store and bought a sandwich. Then we went home and made love for the first time in four months.

I was still not entirely free, though, since part of my sentence included four months of house arrest and two years of probation. I couldn't go anywhere without permission, although I did get a job at Ford's Colony. The patriarch was gracious enough to tell me, "When you get out, if you are allowed to have a job, I would be more than happy to employ you. You've lived here a long time and you're a good person. I know that, we all know that. We will be more than happy to employ you." And that's what he did. I worked in and around the pro shop and golf course. But that was the only time I could leave the house. I even had to wear a monitor, which started out as a watch-type device and later was an ankle bracelet. Everybody saw it since I wore shorts a lot. I also worked as a ranger a little bit. What I did was to make sure the group in front of me played fast enough and I made sure that the group behind me stayed up.

Ford's Colony got me out of the house but I didn't do any traveling. I was able to go to a job, go to the doctor, or go to the store. I had certain hours that I could work but I had to submit a schedule to an officer of the court. I did it without any issues or problems whatsoever for the four months.

Since I was home so much, with time on my hands, I also launched a website for people facing the same situation I had been in. It was called www.areyoureadyforjail.com. My intent was to give information to people who never thought they would be in a situation similar to mine—primarily white-collar workers who made a mistake. I wanted to tell them what they were getting into, or what they were being *thrown* into, and also how to help their families and ease some of the anxiety that they were feeling. To say it's an intense time before incarceration is certainly an understatement.

Fear of the unknown is tremendous. My goal was to talk to these people and tell them that, even though they're incarcerated, they are protected by the system. They weren't going to a torture chamber. And they didn't have to be fearful of the facility. My message was simple: if you temper your anger, keep your mouth shut, and don't piss off the wrong people, you really have nothing to fear. Because nobody's gonna fuck with you if you don't fuck with them. The consequences for causing trouble were too severe.

It's kind of a funny culture; after you talk to people, and after you've been around people who have been incarcerated, you get out, you go on, you go back to your previous life, and you never hear from those people again. Not everybody who goes to jail is a bad person or a criminal. A lot of people who go to jail made a mistake and have to pay for it. But the length of their sentence—"the bit," as we called it—shouldn't define who they are if they've been a good person before and they're going to be a good person afterward. It was just something that happened in their lives.

People would call, leave a credit card number, and I would talk to them, whether it be once or ten times, for a fee. The people who were in touch were probably not criminals but people who made a mistake and had to pay for it, as I had. I gave them advice based upon my own experience. I eased their fears.

As in so many other situations in my life, as an umpire and as a person, it was okay to help people. It was okay to say that the situation may be unknown but is not as bad as you think it is. It would be worse if you didn't adhere to the rules, if you didn't know what was going on before you got there. Talking to someone who had been there was an important part of coping with getting ready to go. It helped a lot of people. I had men and women call me while they were incarcerated to thank me—and thank me again after they got out, telling me there should be more services like mine.

The only person with whom I stayed a little bit friendly was T. He was there for about two years after I left. I sent him some funds every month so he could buy whatever he needed in the commissary once a week. When he got out, he went back to Washington DC and I tried to help him get a job there. He showed up for the interview and supposedly got the job but never showed up for it. I never heard from him again.

The situation was bad and the memories are tough but being incarcerated was a tremendous learning experience. I would not suggest anyone volunteer for it, but it's probably not the worst thing that's ever happened to me. It's something that happened along the way. It's something I had to deal with. I refuse, absolutely refuse, to allow those four months of incarceration to define my sixty-six years on this planet. It happened, I accepted it, I paid the price, I followed the rules, I got out, and I turned the page.

18 Lasting Impressions

Since I came from a journalistic background, I always read the newspapers every day, no matter what city I was in. I wanted to know which writers were biased or unbiased, professional journalists or shills.

My dad, Herb, was a biased writer, but only when covering the Yankees. Like so many beat writers in the big leagues who were intimidated by the ball clubs they covered, he believed if he wrote anything negative he would be denied access that was essential to writing good stories. Herb was not only a longtime member of the Baseball Writers Association of America but a lifelong Yankee fan to boot. As a BBWAA member, he had the privilege of voting for players who qualified for the Hall of Fame. But, like so many other writers, he had a twisted view of the voting process. My dad voted only for Yankees or former Yankees when they became eligible. He and I heartily disagreed about that but, until his dying day, he found it very difficult to vote for anyone else. He did finally vote for Jim Rice after I convinced him he was a Hall of Famer, but very few others.

The Hall of Fame election system probably should be changed, but it's not my business. It's tough to get 75 percent of the vote. But I've got no say in it, no skin in the game. Whatever the baseball writers want to do, as hypocritical as it might be, is okay. I've got one steadfast and subjective opinion about the Hall: I don't think it will be complete until Pete Rose is a member. If or when that's going to happen, I have no idea. But I just think that the career hits leader should be acknowledged in the Hall of Fame. He earned the name Charlie Hustle for a reason. Any manager would have loved to have nine guys like Pete on the field.

The Barry Bonds situation is different. The steroids era will certainly have some kind of asterisk near it because those players cheated in the game. As far as we know, Rose never juiced. He gambled on games but supposedly only as a manager, never while playing. Gambling of any kind in the game has always been taboo. Remember the 1919 Black Sox scandal and the movie *Eight Men Out*?

Bonds, Roger Clemens, and the others implicated or accused in the steroids era have been depicted as using performance enhancing drugs (PED), supposedly to help them recover more quickly, become stronger, and give them an unfair advantage over their peers. Should Bonds be in the Hall of Fame? I'm of the opinion that, like Rose, there should be some acknowledgment of his accomplishments. Should there be an asterisk? Maybe there should be a separate wing in the Hall for the stars of the steroids era. The same goes for Clemens. I'm a big believer in the court system: he's innocent until proven guilty, or admits his guilt the way Mark McGwire did. Mark worked hard but, by his own admission, used performance-enhancing drugs prohibited by baseball. Players who use performance-enhancing drugs are cheating.

As is the case in judging presidents, history should be the decider rather than immediate snap decisions. It's going to take another couple of decades, perhaps, to see where the baseball stats stand when no one is using steroids. You've got to look at each individual case. Clemens had a work ethic that was perhaps unparalleled. He worked hard to get ready to pitch. I'm not sure it's accurate to say that anybody who plays that long has some kind of artificial assistance. Nolan Ryan played in the Major Leagues for twenty-seven years but nobody ever accused him of juicing.

Cheating goes far beyond drug abuse. Since the game began 150 years ago, pitchers have parlayed trick pitches, slippery substances, and various other tools into an arsenal that they deployed against enemy hitters. The spitball was banned in 1920 but some pitchers continued to use it. Many umpires who saw Don Sutton suspected he was cheating. We suspected Tommy John, too. I'm not referring to steroids at all. I'm talking about scuffing the ball. By scuffing a baseball on one side and then throwing it, the vacuum created by the air is altered so that the ball moves sharply one way or the other. Joe Niekro hid a nail file in his back pocket and got caught, ejected, and fined.

Then there was Gaylord Perry, who was such an obvious suspect that umpires practically made him undress on the mound. It was a psychological thing. Everybody *thought* he cheated, so perception became truth. If a hitter thought that a pitcher was doing it, that was as good as him actually cheating. If a batter goes up to hit with the idea that Perry (or anybody) was doing something wrong, that interfered with his concentration. Advantage pitcher.

I never started umpiring a game with a preconceived notion about what a pitcher might be doing. We play today's game today and handle any given situation if and when it occurs.

The only time umpires are officially aware of previous incidents between two teams is when the crew is notified by supervisors in the commissioner's office that there was a bone of contention—usually a beanball or sign-stealing incident—between those particular clubs. Forewarned was forearmed. The best way to stop trouble before it began was to inform the managers at home plate during the exchange of lineup cards that we were aware of what happened previously. Seldom do umpires issue warnings before a game. But if the clubs know that the umpires are aware of a potential problem, the issue might be tempered before boiling over.

Doug Harvey, a National League umpire for many years, was a master at cooling things down. Players and coaches had so much respect for him that his nickname was God. Many young umpires learned valuable lessons from simply walking on the field with him. There aren't many umpires in Cooperstown, but

Harvey is one of them. He was selected by the Veterans Committee, the only group that can select umpires for enshrinement in the Hall of Fame.

After spending parts of four decades in baseball, I've developed my own criteria for a players' enshrinement. I do not believe players from different eras should be compared with or pitted in statistical competition against each other. I do believe, however, that if a player made a difference in the era in which he performed, he should be elected by the Baseball Writers' Association of America. Personality seems to get in the way too often.

Two perfect examples are Mike Schmidt and Jim Rice. Schmidt was elected in his first year of his eligibility. Rice wasn't chosen until his fifteenth and last year on the ballot. Yet during their most productive years, Schmidt and Rice were the two most prolific offensive players in their leagues. How could Mike Schmidt be elected on the first ballot and Jim Rice not get in until his fifteenth? The only explanation is Mike was a gracious guy with the media and Jim was not. Rice was a little moody. But should that be a consideration by the writers? Did that detract from his Hall of Fame credentials? I don't think so.

Whether they are retired or active, players who use performance-enhancing drugs are cheating. They shouldn't be. Illegal drugs have no place in the game. Let the best teams and the best players win on their own merits. Advances have been made in technology for training, for getting stronger. I just don't believe performance-enhancing drugs should be part of our game—or our culture.

Every generation has its idiosyncrasies. When Babe Ruth played, Prohibition prevailed but people used alcohol anyway. In the '60s and early '70s, it was amphetamines and chartreuse pills, known as greenies. Then we had cocaine and later the PEDs.

While the means can always be called into question, players are always looking for ways to make themselves better while still remaining relevant. Satchel Paige said it best: "Don't be looking over your shoulder because somebody might be gaining on you." If a younger player is gaining and you're the person who is getting a little bit older, you're going to be working to stay competitive, to keep playing as long as possible. The dollars earned today—millions and millions a year—make them want to stay in the big leagues as long as they can. Who can blame them?

What happens when you give a twenty-year-old kid millions of dollars? He doesn't just get his kicks by going to the movies on a Saturday night. He buys a house; buys a vacation house; and takes care of his mom, dad, and siblings. Then what? He buys all the cars he wants. Checks keep coming in. The money players earn can be detrimental to their health when they're young. They think they are Teflonized, not responsible for their own actions. Nobody says no to them. Someone is always around to say yes without thinking. That includes publicists, restaurant people, business people, and plenty of women. We see it every day in professional sports.

There's pressure to perform at the highest level of competition, but what if you don't? A player has to keep up with expectations; it's too good a lifestyle to leave. I saw that every day. Every single day. The newest phenom would come up and would think that baseball was invented when he got to the big leagues.

Look at Darryl Strawberry and Dwight Gooden, two young players in New York who had fame and money thrust upon them in the go-go 1980s. They were bona fide stars. How good could they have been if they handled their success differently? Those kinds of stories are repeated time and again by young athletes all over the country.

We live in a free enterprise system and society. Players are independent contractors whose shelf life as professional athletes on the big stage is short lived. They should earn whatever the market will bear. If it takes agents to get them a lot of money, so be it. If the baseball club owners couldn't pay the money players are receiving, then they wouldn't pay it. Is it right that they earn that much? It is if you believe in the free enterprise system—but probably is not if you compare those wages to the salaries of teachers, first responders, and perhaps even some doctors.

Athletes and officials are not finding a cure for cancer or solving the world's problems. What we are doing—and it's important—is providing a diversion. Professional sports provide an escape from everyday problems for a whole lot of people. Fifty or sixty million people per year pay their way into countless ballparks, Major League and Minor League, and hundreds of millions watch baseball on television or listen to it on the radio.

Radio is one aspect of the game that has changed dramatically in my view. When I was growing up in Trenton, I listened to Mel Allen and Red Barber broadcast Yankees games. Later on I got to meet them. It was a thrill to meet my boyhood heroes. Many game announcers today couldn't carry the microphones of Ernie Harwell, Jack Buck, Vin Scully, Milo Hamilton, Bob Prince, Russ Hodges, and a host of others. Perhaps it's because of television and the ratings game. I actually had one former announcer tell me he didn't care about accuracy as long as his listeners were happy and sponsors satisfied. It makes me wonder what happened to professional pride.

I wrote my college thesis on sports writing in the twentieth century. As part of my research I wrote Shirley Povich of the *Washington Post*, Joe Falls of the *Detroit Free Press*, Leonard Koppett of the *New York Times*, Dick Young of the *New York Daily News*, and several other well-known columnists. To a man, they all wrote back to me.

I went to the archives and libraries, looked at microfilm of old newspapers, and read their accounts of the games. I loved the way the writers of that era (1920s and '30s) wrote about baseball. The biggest difference between that era and today is the way the writers used adjectives. Because television was not yet common, they would talk about how blue the sky was, how green the grass was, and even how it smelled—just the aroma of fresh-cut grass on the infield. The first baseman was the first-*sacker* because the bases were sacks. I learned so much in researching something I loved. Since my dad was a writer, I was innately drawn. That was such a valuable time.

Years later, when I was umpiring in the big leagues, I saw Shirley Povich in Baltimore when he was scheduled to throw out the first pitch at Camden Yards. His son Maury Povich was there, too, so I asked him if I could talk to his dad for a second. It was just before the game so I was in uniform. Television news personality Connie Chung, Maury's wife, was there and couldn't have been nicer. She was just a peach of a woman. Maury took me over to his dad. I introduced myself and told him I had written to him when I was a college student. I also reminded him that he had written me a two-and-a-half-page letter about sports writing in the twentieth century and what style changes he thought there might be in the future. Even at sixty-six years old I still remember how excited I was when I received Shirley Povich's thoughtful reply. That was rich, just rich. Those old-time writers, like the old-time broadcasters, had so much pride in their work. I think a lot of that has been lost.

The problem I have with media people today is that they don't want to be fair. Their work is slanted, most of it in favor of the club they are covering. That may seem natural, but it also seems very unprofessional. So often in today's games, writers and broadcasters are just shills for the team they are covering. A local broadcaster sounds so different than a national broadcaster. They're not fair—and they root as if they were fans. That's not their job, in my opinion. What happened to the adage "No cheering in the press box"?

If you were a fan of the New York Yankees, you would have loved Phil Rizzuto because all he did was shill for the Yankees. I might be wrong, but I didn't think that was very professional. Local writers were intimidated and wouldn't write anything nasty about the home team because if they did, and somebody from the club read it, they might have their press privileges revoked. Beat writers told slanted stories and wouldn't come into an umpires' dressing room to find out what really happened in a controversial situation. They'd rather go to the player or manager involved, get his take on it and run with it. That's very unfair and unbalanced. Very seldom—almost never—does a member of the media come in to talk to an umpire about what happened on the field, whether it be a controversial play, a good play, or a bad play. Doesn't a professional journalist want to be as correct in his reporting as possible?

Umpires don't care who wins or loses, who does well, or who does not do well. They have no bias whatsoever in carrying out their responsibilities. Therefore, wouldn't it seem logical that if a media member wanted to get the facts, he or she would go to the most unbiased group in the ballpark? That doesn't happen, even though the media is always welcome in the umpires' dressing room. There's no restriction barring the media from coming in and talking about any play or situation. If something big happens, the umpires can go to a press area where more people can be accommodated.

Coming into our little dressing room seemed to pose problems for some media types. In New York, Joe Donnelly of *Newsday* would come in but that didn't surprise us: he had been an amateur umpire in baseball and softball. He not only knew the rulebook but had an understanding of our job. Very few writers said hello on a regular basis. Gerry Fraley, Tracy Ringolsby, John Lowe, and Bob Elliott are a few who did. On the TV side, Jon Miller sometimes came in but very seldom did we see Joe Morgan. Miller was very fair to umpires.

John Kruk, who's with ESPN now, was very sympathetic to the umpires. He didn't give us a hard time. Of course, Kruk was a pretty good player. The good players hardly ever give the umpires a tough time. It was the also-ran players, the players looking over their shoulders, the players who didn't have the confidence in their own ability, the players always trying to make excuses who gave umpires problems. It was always somebody else's fault. Nothing was ever *their* fault.

I remember a conversation with a national telecaster who I thought had the best interests of our game at heart. He hardly ever ripped anybody. That man was Tony Kubek, the former shortstop for the Yankees who later worked as a broadcaster. Tony said to me, "Hey, listen, Al, not all umpires are good umpires, nor do they get everything right. But our game is strong, and the threads of our game are strong. We who have been in the game don't have to rip people by name." Tony explained to me that when he was on the air and an umpire made a good call or hustled to be in the right position, he always used the umpire's name. When an umpire made a bad call, or what was perceived to be a bad call, he would say only, "the umpire." I thought that was quite professional. He made his point by reporting the truth and was unbiased at the same time.

Harold Reynolds, the former infielder, would always visit with the umpires. He's got an infectious smile and he's a good guy. He was one of the good guys as a player, too.

A frequent visitor to the umpires' dressing room in Detroit was Tigers broadcaster Ernie Harwell. He would just stop by for a minute to say hello and ask how we were. There was nothing special on his mind. He was just a nice man being a nice man.

Detroit baseball fans were the luckiest radio listeners in the world. Ernie, better than anybody else, could draw pictures with words. On a daily basis, Ernie would add such great atmosphere to his broadcasts. After a batter fouled a pitch into the stands, Ernie would say something like, "The pitch is fouled behind the Tiger dugout. And whaddya know? There's Bill Johnson from Ann Arbor in the ballpark today. It's good to see Bill here. It's good to see everybody from Ann Arbor here."

Ernie would pick out names even though he didn't actually know who was catching the foul balls. What a nice idea. And what a way to promote the cities in Michigan, in Detroit and at the ballpark.

Listening to Ernie was magical, and I tried to tune in to his broadcasts as often as possible. Once I was driving after a ballgame in Cleveland, listening to Ernie call the Tigers game from the West Coast. On a ball hit to Alan Trammell's right, he said, "Two-hopper to Trammell's right. Alan backhands it, pirouettes, throws a strike to first base, and nips the runner by a half-step." I could visualize the baseball ballet he described—even though the actual play was probably nothing more than a routine grounder to short.

Ernie was a multitalented southern gentleman, a fine writer, and published songwriter. He was also a genteel, gentle man. He never had a bad word to say about anybody. The statue of him at Comerica Park is a tremendous tribute.

Vin Scully was the ultimate professional. He would speak differently on a national telecast or broadcast than he would when he was with the Dodgers in Los Angeles. If he was speaking to his Los Angeles audience, he would be very biased and pro–Los Angeles. But when he was on a national telecast or broadcast, he was as professional as professional can be. He would give both sides to a story, and laud a good play by either team's players. You don't find that very often anymore.

I thought about being a broadcaster, too. I've been told I have a good voice and I would've liked doing it. But the opportunity never presented itself. And I wanted to be on the field. Besides, if I had become a broadcaster, I would've had to leave home again, and I love where I live.

The location was perfect for me. It afforded me three airports to use while I was still working: Richmond, Newport News, and Norfolk. Since I'm living in the Mid-Atlantic states, I still have the change of seasons.

My home is in Ford's Colony, a gated community with fifty-four holes of golf in beautiful colonial Williamsburg. I finally achieved an elusive hole in one last summer. Scoring an ace, as it's called in golf, is roughly equivalent to hitting for the cycle in baseball. It happens only once in a blue moon.

In addition to my golf clubs, I found room in my life for several pets. I love animals almost as much as I love kids. It's too late in my life to start raising a family now, but it's never too late for pets. I find them to be great company. I still have Marty, a gold-colored indoor/outdoor cat, and Bella, a small white dog who sometimes sits on my shoulder. She's a Maltese and Bichon Frisé mix.

I relax by reading the newspaper every day and reading books about history, historical figures, fiction, and anything by James Patterson or John Grisham.

I love music, especially jazz and progressive jazz. I love instrumentals and listen to them all the time. I'm a fan of Bruce Hornsby, who happens to be from Williamsburg.

In addition to sports I like to watch cop and medical shows on television.

I like James Bond films and other action movies. *The Shawshank Redemption* was terrific, and I liked the Ernest Borgnine movie *Marty*, which won an Oscar.

When I do travel, I enjoy public speaking, especially giving after-dinner talks filled with anecdotes. I also give motivational talks to groups about redemption—how to find your way again after life throws you a curve.

I've worked for Busch Gardens Williamsburg and Sports Travel and Tours, a company that runs group baseball trips out of Hatfield, Massachusetts. I also do consulting and public speaking through my own company, Al Clark Enterprises, LLC.

I stopped smoking about eight or nine years ago so my house is smoke free. Tobacco is one of the most addictive agents ever. I wanted to stop smoking but knew I needed help. So I went to my doctor, told him of my plight, and was prescribed Centrex, which cost about $130 for a month's supply. I was determined.

I also managed to stop drinking. I had been drinking in the evening after games but never before games. I made a promise to myself while in the low Minor Leagues that I would never ever drink alcohol—not even a beer with lunch and a sandwich—on days when I was working at night. That's a promise I kept for twenty-six years in the big leagues and four years in the Minors. I never slipped, not one time. It was a different story after a game. I had been drunk as far as five miles up in an airplane and as low as many hotel basements and a lot of places in between.

Looking back, I admit that I had a lot of fun with alcohol and drinking—as do a whole lot of people. I just decided, quite honestly, that there wasn't anything left for me in a bottle of alcohol. My career was over. So I woke up one day and stopped drinking. Just like that. Cold turkey. I said to myself, "I'm done." And because of that, I am now the best designated driver in all of Williamsburg, Virginia. I go to parties, I go to bars, I go to any place that has alcohol. I'll drink my club soda, I'll drink iced tea, I'll drink a diet soda, and it doesn't bother me in the least.

I am still the same fun-loving guy, only sober and smoke-free. Tobacco and alcohol are addictive and I didn't need them in my life. What I do need are my memories of things I have experienced. For example, I was an extra on the NBC soap opera *Santa Barbara* three years in a row.

I had always enjoyed watching that show. In fact, I liked it so much that I called Michael Weissman, executive producer of NBC Sports. I had met him a number of times because NBC then had the Game of the Week—the only baseball game televised nationally. When I got Michael on the phone, I said, "I'd like to go to your Burbank studios, get on the set, and meet the people of *Santa Barbara*." Michael, being totally ensconced in the sports world, asked, "Al, what the hell is *Santa Barbara*?" I told him it was one of NBC's soap operas. It was springtime and he said, "I'm going to Paris for the French Open, but I'll give you the name of my assistant." I could hear him talking to her, and she set up a visit to the show's set in California.

Every time I went to Anaheim for the next couple of years, I journeyed to NBC's Burbank studios and was welcomed onto the soap opera's set. At various points I played a police officer , a bar patron, and a person eating in a nice restaurant. I even had a speaking part once; I was the maître d' in a restaurant. That was pretty much the extent of my acting career.

I was also in a Chevy Chase comedy called *National Lampoon's European Vacation*. During the credits there was a scene of the Griswolds coming back to the United States. They flew over Yankee Stadium, where there was an argument going on between Dave Winfield and me over a play at home plate. Of course Winnie was wrong and I was right.

Movie stars, politicians, and other celebrities always seemed to be around the ballpark. Since I was on the field, I met many of them. I had the good fortune to shake hands with every president in office during my time in Major League Baseball. Canadian prime ministers also dropped into the umpires' dressing room on occasion. Actor Tom Selleck loves baseball, but especially the Detroit Tigers. We chatted at Tiger Stadium whenever our paths crossed and he asked me to be a consultant on his film *Mr. Baseball*. He later sent me a *Mr. Baseball* belt buckle inscribed with a note on the back. That was a nice souvenir. I got to meet many other celebrities over the years, too.

Baseball has changed a lot since I reached the Majors in 1976. The biggest changes were the introduction of three-division play and the wild-card winner, then the addition of the second wild-card team in 2012.

If the wild-card game increases the popularity of the game and keeps interest up in September, where games are significant in so many more cities, maybe it's not so bad. It's always a barroom argument between the traditionalists and the younger crowd. There was a time when baseball was not played west of the Mississippi. But times change. It's called progress, I guess.

Anything that promotes our game, creates interest, puts more people in the stands, and keeps football off the front page of the sports section in September is good for our game. If more divisions and more playoff games do that, so be it. The game is for the fans; if the fans like it, and think it is a positive change, why not do it?

Discussion is good. Remember the talk of the asterisk when Roger Maris hit sixty-one home runs in 1961? The schedule was 154 games long when Babe Ruth hit sixty but when Roger broke his record, he had a 162-game schedule. Things change. We have to adapt.

Umpires had to change, too. Instead of being American and National League umpires, we became Major League umpires.

Change is inevitable. It is always progress? Not necessarily. But change is going to happen. It's like time; it just keeps on moving.

For me, the one thing that never changed was my interaction with the fans at the ballpark. I loved talking to baseball fans. Whenever I worked first or third base, I'd always walk over to the stands between innings. There were usually season-ticket holders sitting up front, so you'd see the same people year in and year out. You'd say, "Hello, it's nice to see you. Are you having a good year?" Just something to make the game experience a little more personal, a little more touchable, a little more reachable.

I especially loved dealing with kids. Kids were amazing at the ballpark. Whenever I walked over to the railing, many youngsters gathered immediately. I would talk to the kids, I would high-five with the kids. Usually I'd take a baseball with me, one that would have been thrown out. If there was a youngster with a glove, I'd ask to see his glove. I would put the ball in his glove and then, without telling him, give the glove back to him. He would look down at the baseball and then look at me and his eyes would get as big and as white as the baseball in his glove. It's a moment that youngster would probably never forget. How is he not now a paying customer all his life?

Sometimes I'd take a baseball over and show it to all the kids. I'd lean over with my right sleeve and show them my number 24.

I'd say to them, "One of you guys is going to get this baseball." I told them the way to earn it was to guess a number between fifteen and thirty. All the while, my number 24 would be staring them right in the face. All the adults would get it immediately. But I'd let only the kids guess. I'd go from one to another, the shortest to the tallest or the youngest to the oldest. Finally someone would look at my number and blurt out, "Twenty-four." I'd give the baseball to the youngster and the rest of the kids would go, "Awwww, gee." It was fun to interact with both the kids and adults at the ballpark. It created a great public relations moment for baseball, for the ballpark, and for the team. It was an absolute win-win deal.

Baseball fans are notorious for knowing the people in their game. They recognize umpires walking down the street in Chicago, Kansas City, Boston, New York, and Philadelphia. That's true even today, although umpires don't get to all the cities as often as we once did. If you never get out of your hotel, you don't get to know the flavor of the fans in that particular city, nor do you have the opportunity to become friends with the people.

One thing I learned early on is that there are so many more good people in our country than bad people. If I made a controversial call the night before and was recognized the next day, I was never confronted on the street by a fan who recognized me. The conversation was always cordial; the fan would want to talk about the game and to know what happened on the field and why. I loved to talk with the fans, whether it was at the ballpark, in restaurants, or on the street. That was a great fun part of being on the road.

A pleasant conversation was always a nice interlude; as umpires we were used to forty or fifty thousand people booing us. The accolades were welcome, but so was the booing. It came with the territory and with the uniform. We were trained to accept that, deal with it, and understand the mentality of the crowd.

One thing I had trouble accepting was going to prison. I don't think I was dealt with fairly. This has nothing to do with baseball. I think the legal system, in some regards, is a fraud itself. Prosecutors and courts will pick and choose whom they want to go after. Prosecutors who want to make a name for themselves will go after a more high-profile person. I don't mean that to be a demeaning statement about a particular prosecutor; that's just the way the legal system is. That's the way that I see it. I've got no basis for saying that, other than my own opinion, but I'm allowed to have one.

I feel strongly that baseball should be able to police itself and should dole out more severe punishments to violators. If a player cheats, he shouldn't be able to play. And I'm using myself as an example. I did something wrong, terribly wrong. I broke the rules, and I paid a hefty price. There was no second chance for me from the commissioner's office. So naturally, I take it personally.

Being incarcerated was not the worst thing that ever happened to me. A lot of situations were far worse. Being divorced twice, for example. Family is very, very important. I think that the devastation of not having successful marriages is far worse than four months of being incarcerated. And also much worse than losing a career.

Losing my mother and father was difficult, too. Friends of mine have passed away. Some of them were good friends who passed away before their time from sudden death or disease. That's much harder to deal with than being incarcerated for four months.

Even having to fight for the reputation I've lost is not difficult. Stuff happens. It's life. It happened. It's not the negative things that really define you; it's how you handle them. It's what you learn from them. It's how you try to help others. What kind of character do you have after something negative occurs? Are you willing to hold your head up high?

I made a mistake. I did something I shouldn't have done. I thought I was doing something to help somebody. I didn't gain from it financially at all. And I certainly lost a whole lot because of the decisions I made. But, you know, so what? The people who know me know what kind of person I am. I don't care about the people who want to judge me negatively because I made a mistake.

Through all the acrimony, all the ups and downs that I've experienced, I've got to say my life has been very rich—not because of the money I've earned but because of the friendships I've made all over the country. There isn't a major city I can go to where I would be stranded. I have friends everywhere and because of that I think I am tremendously rich.

I've learned that the best word in the English language is *security*, peace of mind. I've learned that it doesn't matter how great a station one enjoys in life. That's not really important because at the end of the day, we're all just people. What counts most are the people in your life whom you love and who love you. After that—well, there *is no* after that.

Epilogue

This project has been both enlightening and cathartic. It's been enlightening because it's given me the opportunity to review my life, both personally and professionally; to categorize what's been important; and to place perspective on occurrences. It's been cathartic because it's allowed me look with clarity on my past. I'm happy, satisfied, and content with the past sixty-six years.

The time I spent incarcerated taught me patience. The bit also made it clear we all have choices to make and there are benefits or consequences with each one.

In my master bath, on the mirror just above eye level, is my federal prison identification number, 26147-050. Taped there since the day of my release, it was posted for me to see either consciously or subconsciously every day. It's a reminder that the decisions and choices I make today will have effects. I know the only time that number can be active again is if I make a very wrong decision. That is *not* going to happen.

My message is simple: be aware of each and every decision you make. That choice is going to affect you or someone else positively or negatively. Think it through and make the right choice!

Appendix

Full name: Alan Marshall Clark
Born: January 9, 1948, Trenton, New Jersey
Umpired first game: April 9, 1976
Umpired final game: June 13, 2001
Height: 5'10"
Weight: 247

Umpiring Record

Year	LG	G	HP	1B	2B	3B	LF	RF
1976	AL	160	40	40	40	40	0	0
1977	AL	164	42	43	38	41	0	0
1978	AL	147	38	38	36	35	0	0
1979	AL	111	30	28	27	27	0	0
1980	AL	153	38	41	35	39	0	0
1981	AL	106	27	27	27	25	0	0
1982	AL	144	35	38	37	34	0	0
1983	AL	134	34	34	33	33	0	0
1984	AL	149	38	37	38	36	0	0
1985	AL	139	35	36	34	34	0	0
1986	AL	146	37	37	35	37	0	0
1987	AL	150	39	39	35	37	0	0
1988	AL	141	36	34	38	33	0	0
1989	AL	144	36	33	36	39	0	0
1990	AL	141	32	38	34	37	0	0
1991	AL	135	35	33	33	34	0	0
1992	AL	140	35	35	35	35	0	0
1993	AL	127	31	33	31	32	0	0
1994	AL	88	23	22	22	21	0	0
1995	AL	114	28	27	28	31	0	0
1996	AL	127	33	34	28	32	0	0
1997	AL	127	33	31	32	31	0	0

1998	AL	123	32	31	31	29	0	0
1999	AL	103	28	24	24	27	0	0
2000	ML	125	31	31	32	31	0	0
2001	ML	54	13	14	14	13	0	0
Total (26 Years):		3392	859	858	833	843	0	0

Division Series Umpiring Record

Year	LG	G	HP	1B	2B	3B	LF	RF
1981	AL	5	1	1	1	1	1	0
1996	AL	4	0	1	1	1	1	0
2000	ML	3	0	0	1	1	1	0
Total (3 Years):		12	1	2	3	3	3	0

League Championship Series Umpiring Record

Year	LG	G	HP	1B	2B	3B	LF	RF
1979	AL	4	0	1	1	1	1	0
1982	AL	5	0	1	1	1	1	1
1987	AL	5	1	1	1	1	0	1
1992	AL	6	1	1	1	1	1	1
1999	AL	5	1	1	1	1	0	1
Total (5 Years):		25	3	5	5	5	3	4

World Series Umpiring Record

Year	LG	G	HP	1B	2B	3B	LF	RF
1983	ML	5	1	1	1	0	1	1
1989	ML	4	0	1	1	1	1	0
Total (2 Years):		9	1	2	2	1	2	1

All-Star Game Umpiring Record

Year	LG	G	HP	1B	2B	3B	LF	RF
1984	ML	1	0	1	0	0	0	0
1995	ML	1	0	0	1	0	0	0
Total (2 Years):		2	0	1	1	0	0	0

Ejections: 1976 (1), 1977 (5), 1978 (2), 1979 (1), 1980 (3), 1981 (2), 1982 (3), 1983 (4), 1984 (4), 1986 (4), 1987 (2), 1988 (1), 1989 (2), 1990 (2), 1991 (1), 1992 (5), 1993 (4), 1994 (2), 1995 (3), 1996 (5), 1997 (5), 1999 (1), 2000 (3), 2001 (1). Total: 66

Ejection Information

Date	Team	Ejected	Reason
5-21-1976	DET A	Alex Johnson	Call at 1B
4-15-1977	KC A	Whitey Herzog	Interference during DP
4-30-1977	MIN A	Rod Carew	Charging mound after HBP
7-3-1977(2)	TOR A	Otto Velez	Called third strike
8-16-1977	BAL A	Earl Weaver	HBP call (reversal)
9-14-1977(2)	DET A	Lance Parrish	Balls and strikes (while catching)
7-26-1978	BAL A	Jim Frey	Balls and strikes
8-14-1978	MIL A	Gorman Thomas	Call at 2B
5-30-1979	MIL A	George Bamberger	Checked swing
6-8-1980	CAL A	Carney Lansford	Call at 2B (bumped umpire)
6-30-1980	MIN A	Rick Sofield	Call at 3B
10-1-1980	TOR A	John Mayberry	Called third strike
5-27-1981	CHI A	Tony Bernazard	Called third strike (slammed bat)
9-23-1981	MIL A	Don Money	Call at HP from bench
4-13-1982	SEA A	Dave Duncan	Balls and strikes
6-6-1982	OAK A	Billy Martin	Balls and strikes
6-26-1982	NY A	Joe Altobelli	Balls and strikes
5-1-1983	BOS A	Ralph Houk	Balls and strikes
8-8-1983(1)	CHI A	Dave Nelson	Arguing pickoff move was balk
8-9-1983	CHI A	Dave Duncan	Checked swing
9-20-1983	BOS A	Dennis Eckersley	Bench jockeying
6-19-1984	BAL A	John Lowenstein	Balls and strikes
6-27-1984	CHI A	Tony LaRussa	Balk call
7-21-1984	CAL A	Reggie Jackson	Fighting after HBP
9-28-1984	DET A	Chet Lemon	Call at 2B (bumped umpire)
5-26-1986	CAL A	Reggie Jackson	Balls and strikes
7-2-1986	BAL A	Juan Beniquez	Balls and strikes
8-12-1986	TEX A	Pete Incaviglia	Call at 1B
9-21-1986	BAL A	Earl Weaver	Interference call
5-9-1987	TEX A	Mike Loynd	Fighting with Lloyd Moseby
5-9-1987	TOR A	Lloyd Moseby	Charging mound
6-14-1988	BAL A	Frank Robinson	Mimicking umpire (put hands on hips)

6-19-1989	CAL A	Doug Rader	Balls and strikes
9-2-1989	NY A	Roberto Kelly	Balls and strikes
5-21-1990	NY A	Champ Summers	Balls and strikes
9-26-1990	CHI A	Ivan Calderon	Balls and strikes
6-30-1991	CLE A	Felix Fermin	Call at 1B
5-10-1992	CAL A	Luis Polonia	Call at 1B
5-17-1992	NY A	Buck Showalter	Arguing with LaRussa at plate
5-17-1992	OAK A	Tony LaRussa	Arguing with Showalter at plate
8-5-1992	CAL A	Von Hayes	Checked swing
8-21-1992	CAL A	Marcel Lachemann	Bench jockeying
4-8-1993	NY A	Steve Farr	Throwing at Albert Belle
5-11-1993	CLE A	Carlos Martinez	Balls and strikes
7-9-1993	CLE A	Cliff Young	Intentional HBP
7-16-1993	CHI A	Doug Mansolino	After argument with Phil Garner
5-6-1994	OAK A	Steve Sax	Balls and strikes
8-2-1994	CAL A	Bo Jackson	Called third strike
7-8-1995(2)	OAK A	Carney Lansford	Continuing argument between games of DH
7-8-1995(2)	TOR A	Roberto Alomar	Called third strike
9-14-1995	TOR A	Paul Molitor	Checked swing for strike three
6-16-1996	CHI A	Tony Phillips	Balls and strikes
7-23-1996	KC A	Jose Offerman	Called third strike
8-8-1996	CAL A	Chili Davis	Called third strike
8-8-1996	CAL A	John McNamara	Called third strike on Davis
8-17-1996	TOR A	Juan Samuel	Balls and strikes
5-10-1997	CHI A	Ron Jackson	Call at 1B
6-21-1997	CLE A	Johnny Goryl	Balls and strikes
7-6-1997	NY A	Paul O'Neill	Balls and strikes
7-20-1997	BAL A	Cal Ripken	Balls and strikes
8-15-1997(2)	SEA A	Lou Piniella	Call at 3B
6-16-1999	DET A	Gregg Jefferies	Called third strike
4-18-2000	TOR A	John Frascatore	Intentional HBP
4-18-2000	TOR A	Raul Mondesi	Balls and strikes
5-10-2000	ANA A	Mickey Hatcher	Fan interference call
5-27-2001	NY A	Don Zimmer	Bench jockeying